High Shelf

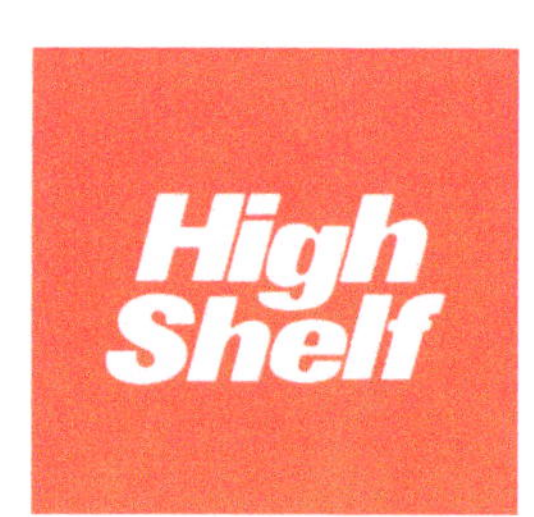

High Shelf Issue XXIII, October 2020.
Portland, Oregon.
Copyright 2020, High Shelf Press

ISBN: 978-1-952869-08-2

Cover Image by Lino Azevedo
Design and Layout by C. M. Tollefson
Edited by David Seung & C. M. Tollefson

With special thanks to:
Kelsey Beck Kuther, Megan Kim, & River Elizabeth Hall.

High Shelf XXIII

October 2020

"...In some cases, you have to break a tooth
and take it out piece by piece
to keep your teeth... "

Natalia Prusinska

"…If you were an infection, what type would you be? I am seriously considering the guillotine. I am pondering the usefulness of the ball-gag. What is your favorite sort of weapon? Mine is your face, after it rains…"
Joanna Acevedo

Table Of Contents

Eyes of the Beholder

Apoorva Prabhakar

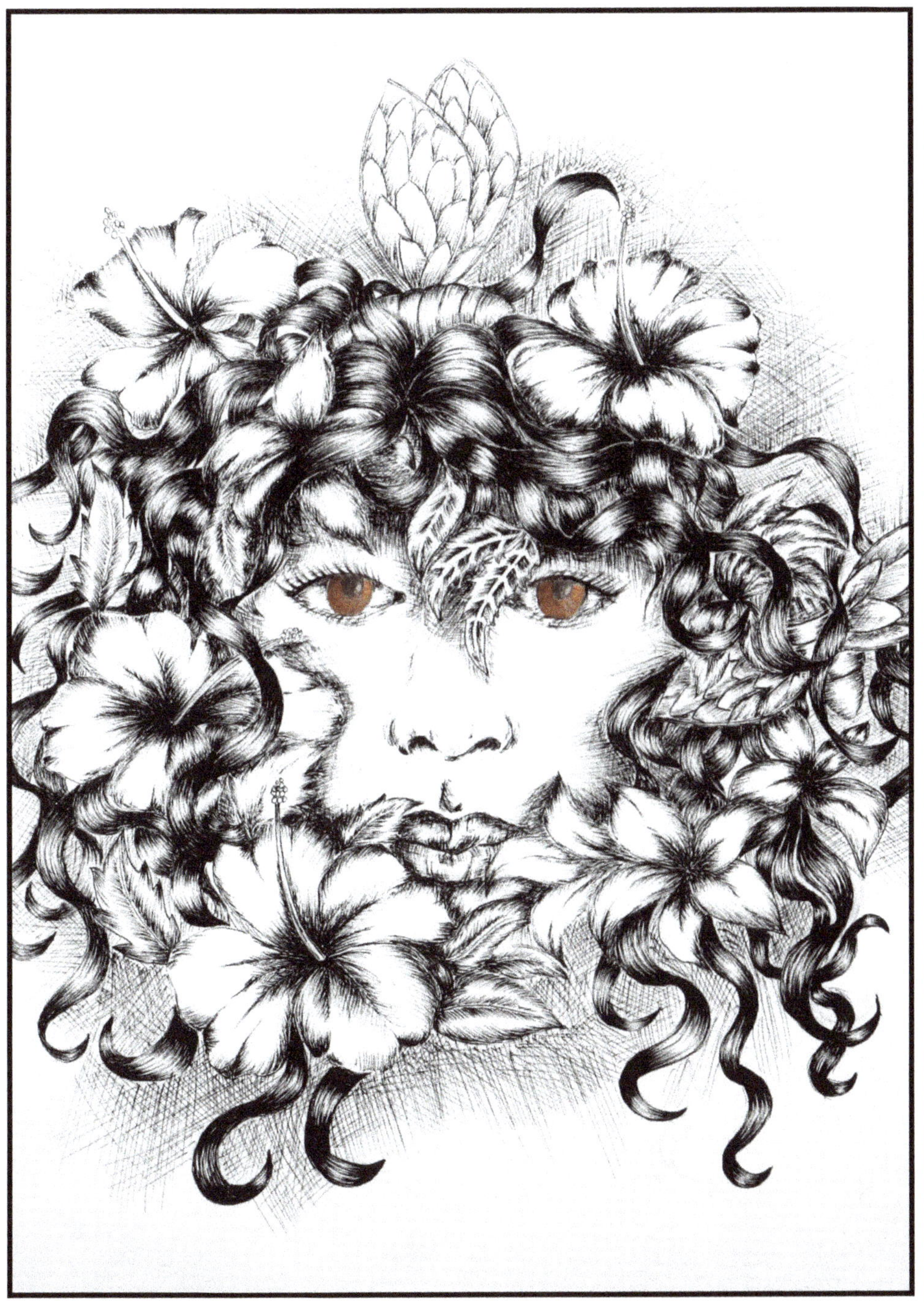

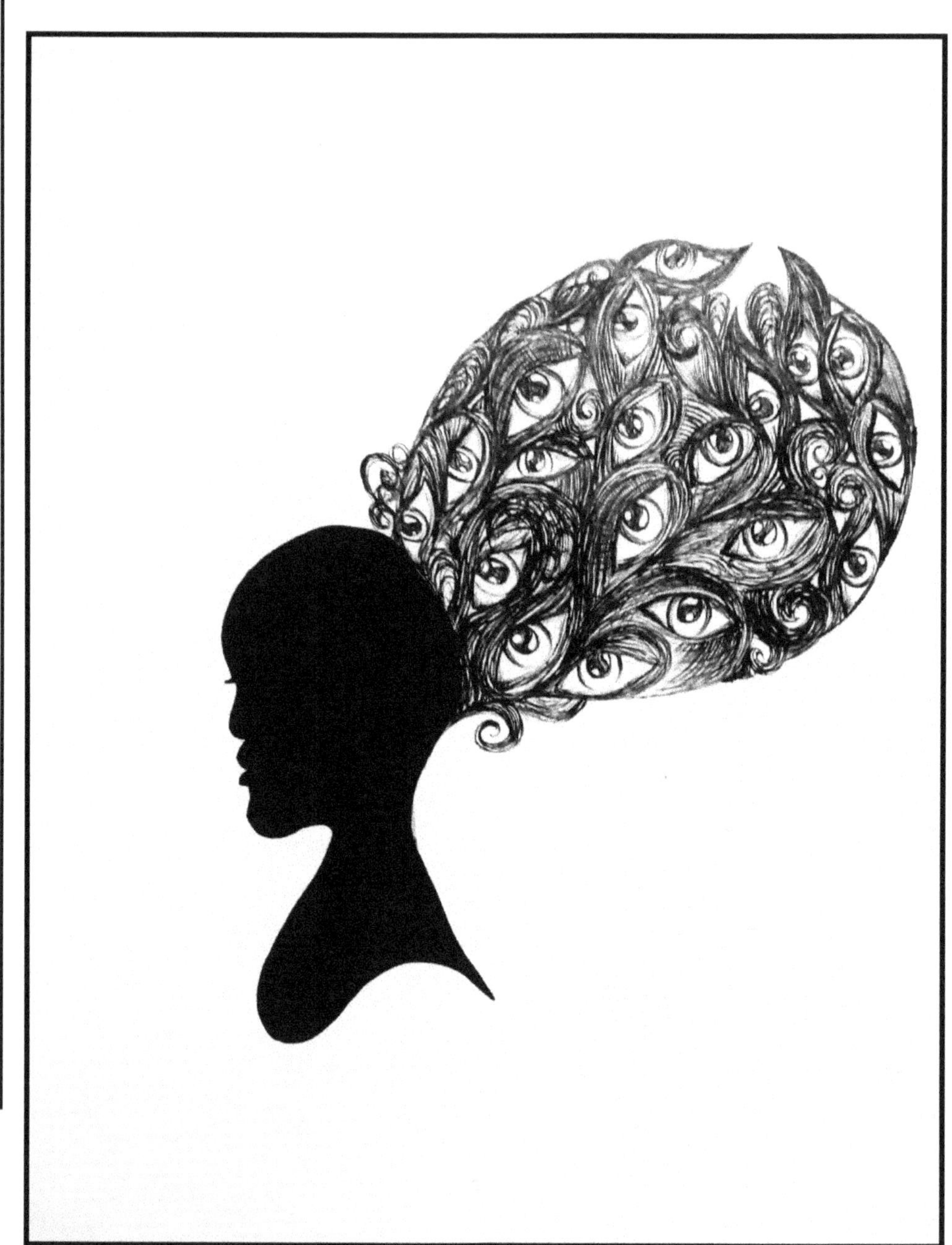

Harbinger

Travis Burkett

grainy footage
grayscale dreamscapes
dust bowl dances
clanging into memory

the messenger crossed
frozen bar ditches
to bring us news
of this reckoning

so we wait here
for the word to thaw
fill our vision like mist
remind of us the sea

PRAY WITH BONES

Laura Lee

You taught me to stop
pray with bones
then move on.

During this day-nighttime
fireflies flash
light the path.

Mother,
I cannot pass;
how beautiful your bones
in the blink-blink gold.

Each Day is a New Ending by Which We Grasp

Natalia Prusinska

I used to store your heart
in the mini fridge next to my bed
along with the probiotics
I always forgot to take.
In some cases, you have to break a tooth
and take it out piece by piece
to keep your teeth
from overcrowding your jaw.
Like how you pull
at the week until it's a month, two months.
Some nights
I pass by thoughts of you,
and catch myself
placing my keys between my knuckles.
Still others, I go to sleep slowly,
happy and aware.

Iterations of Ghosts

Erika Kari McCarthy

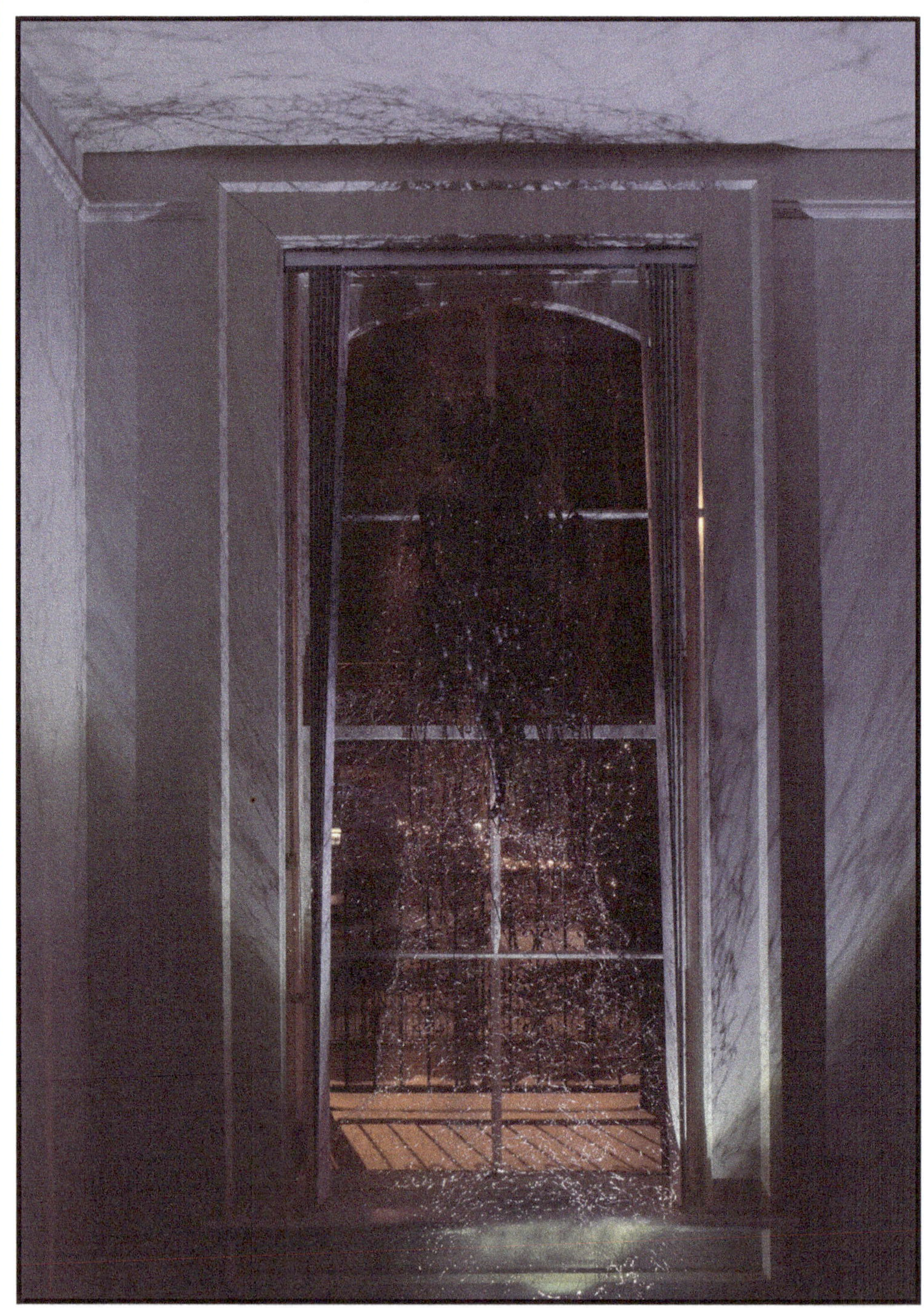

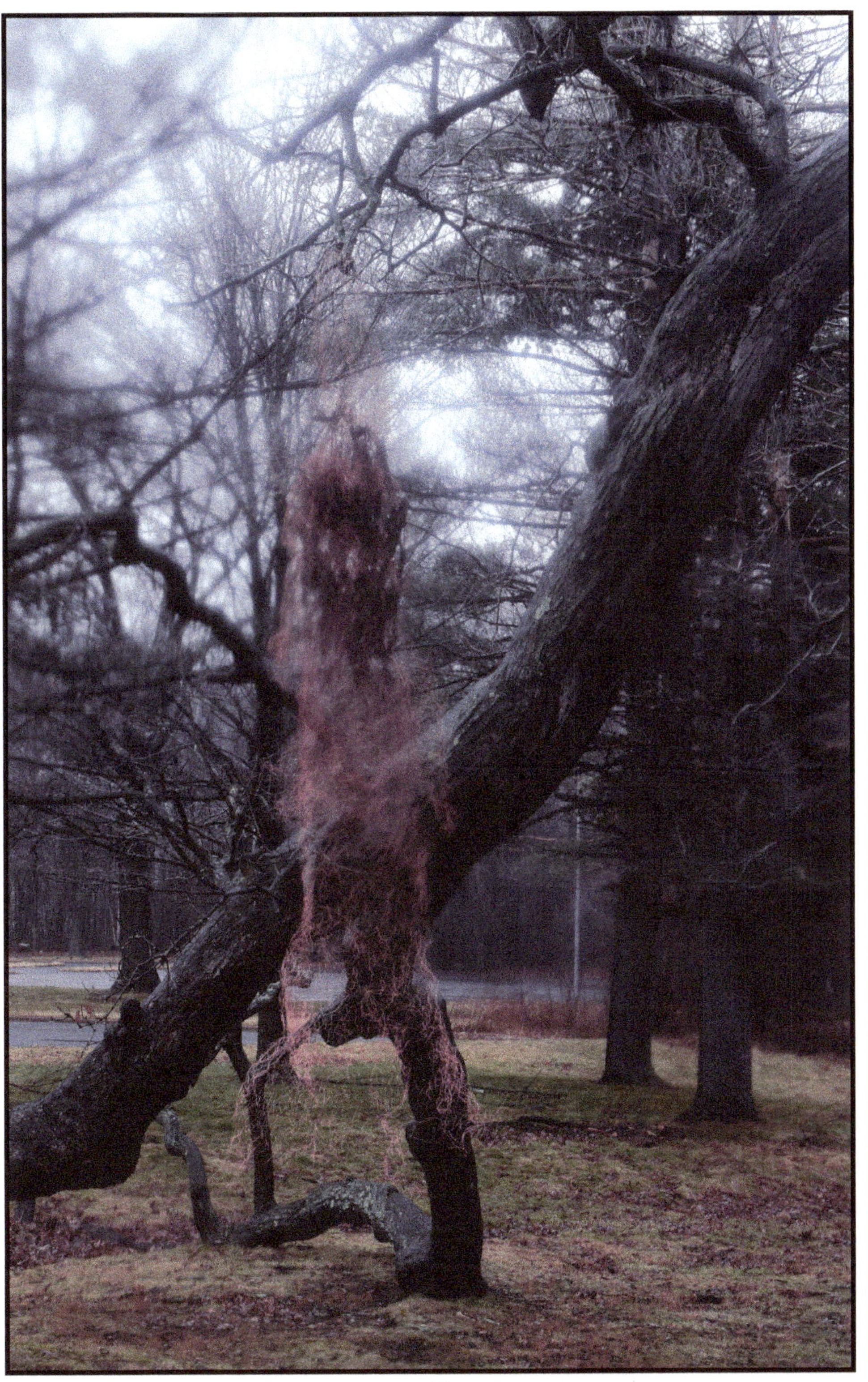

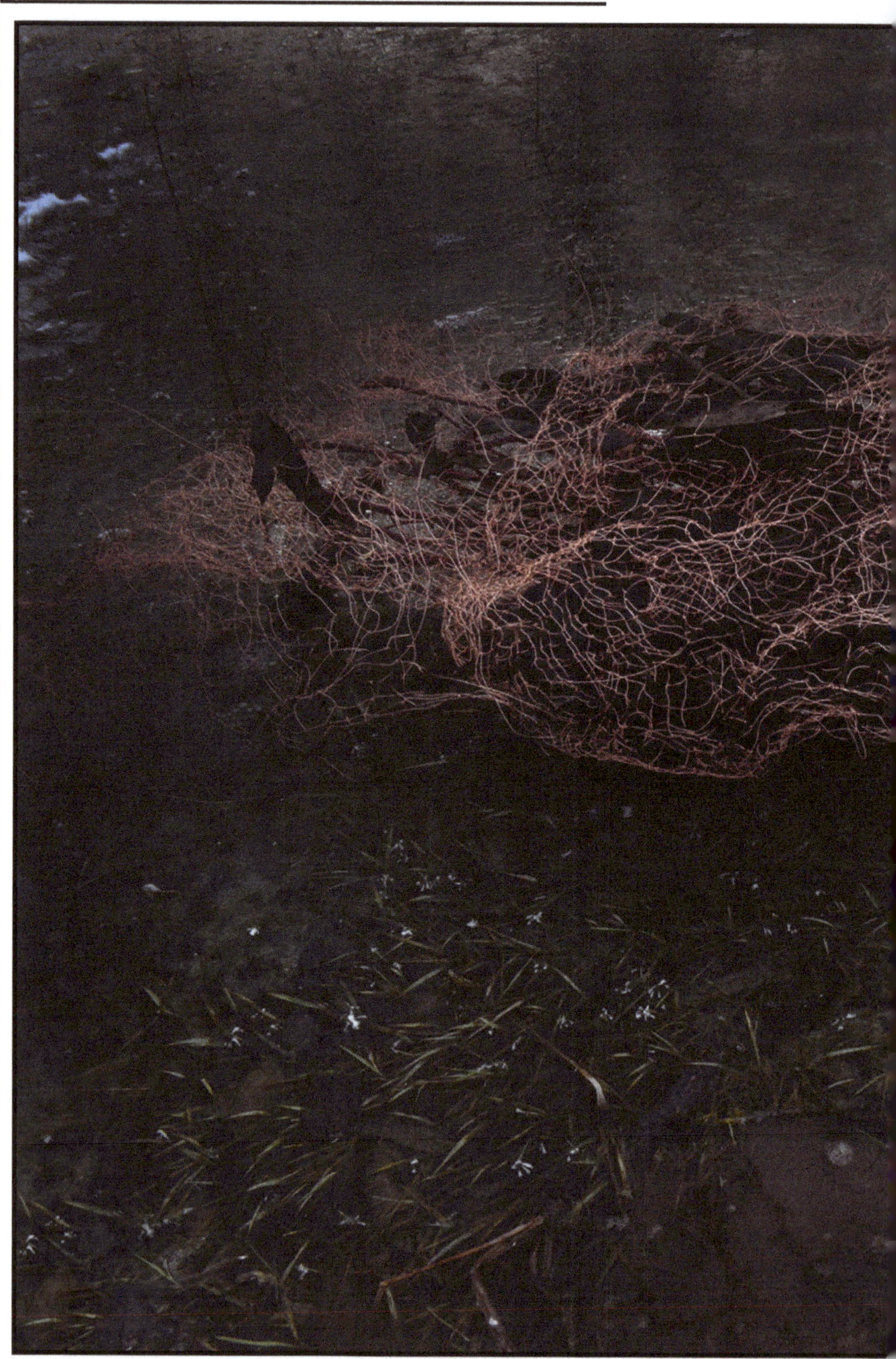

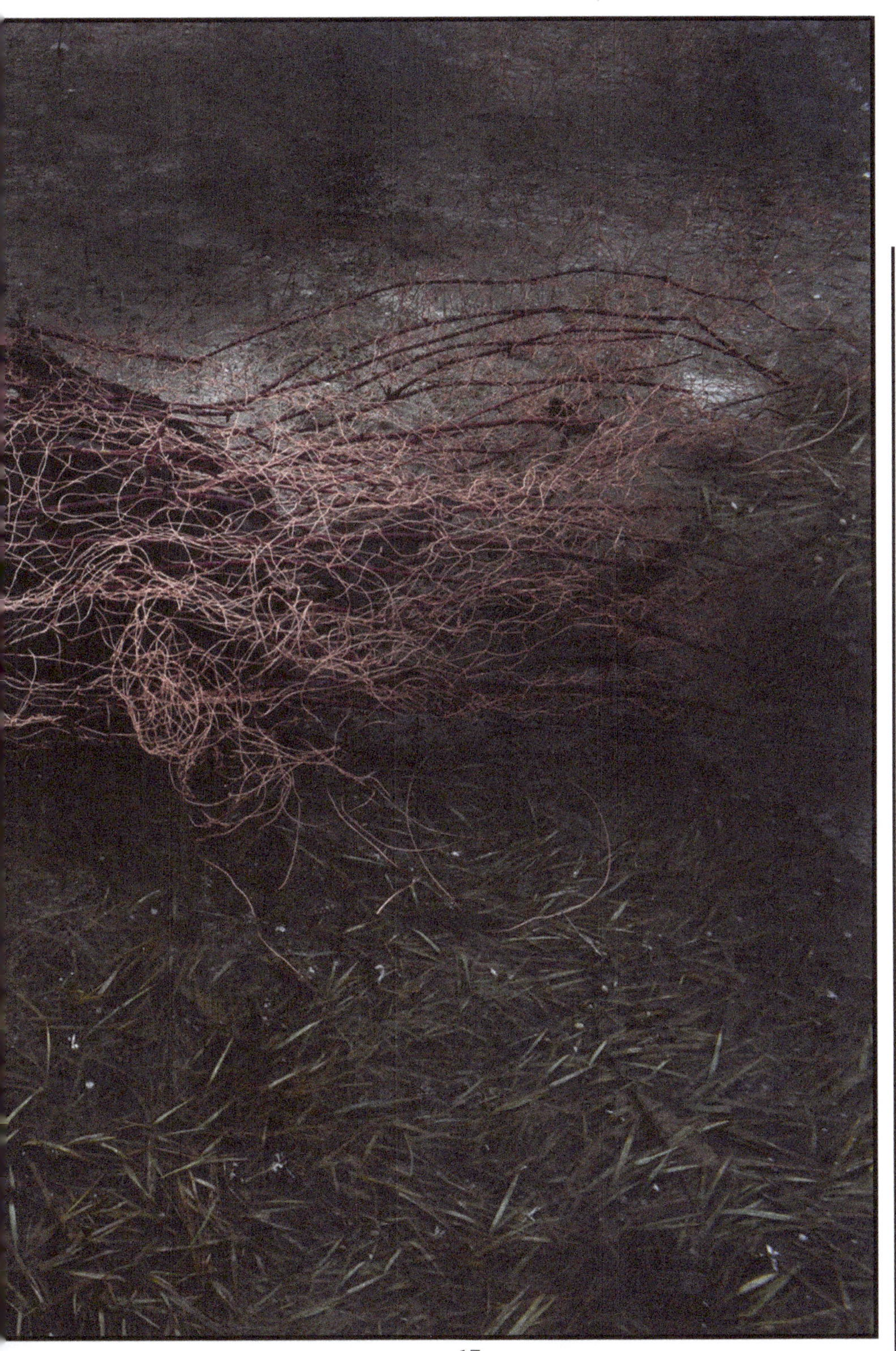

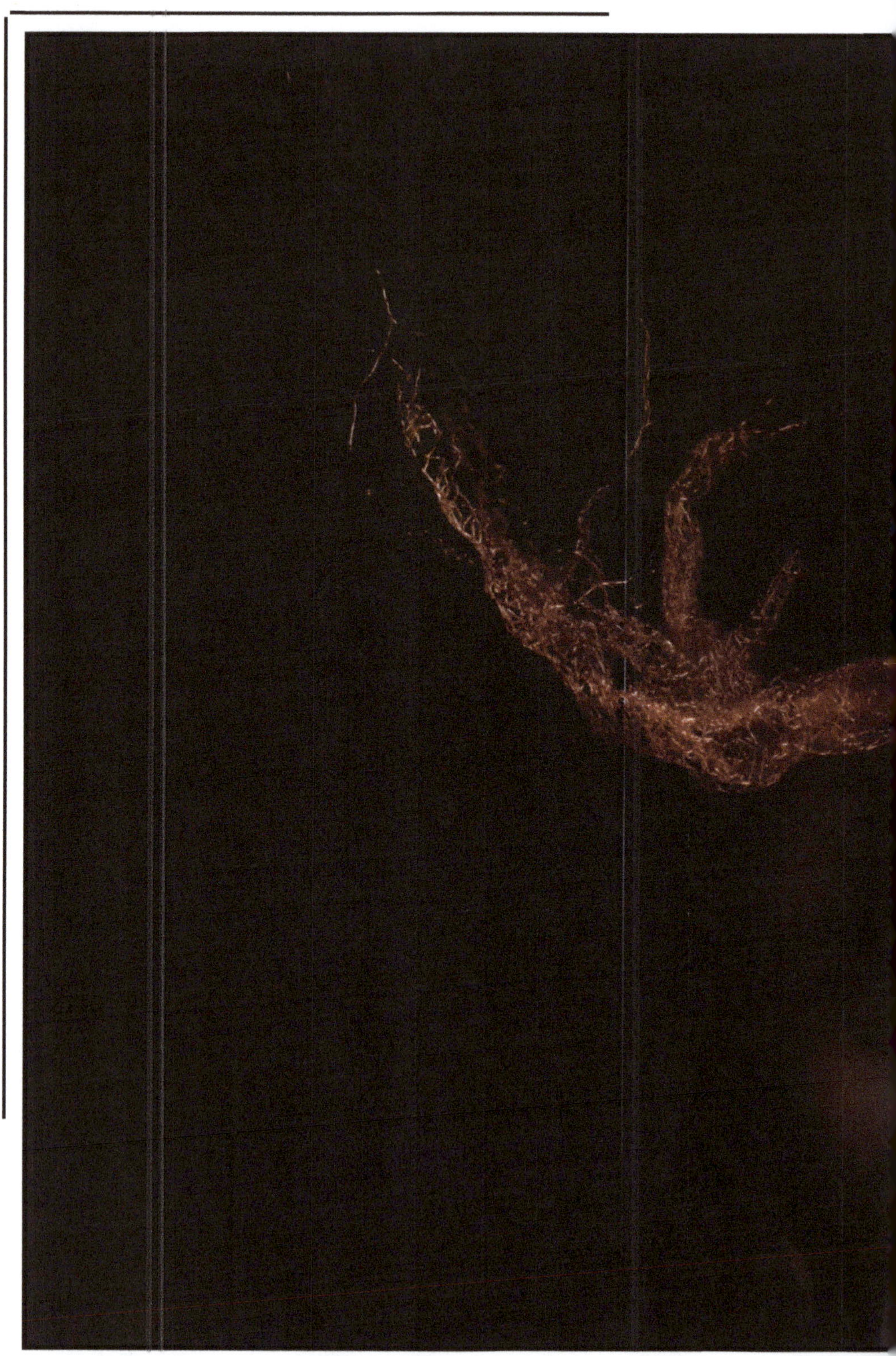

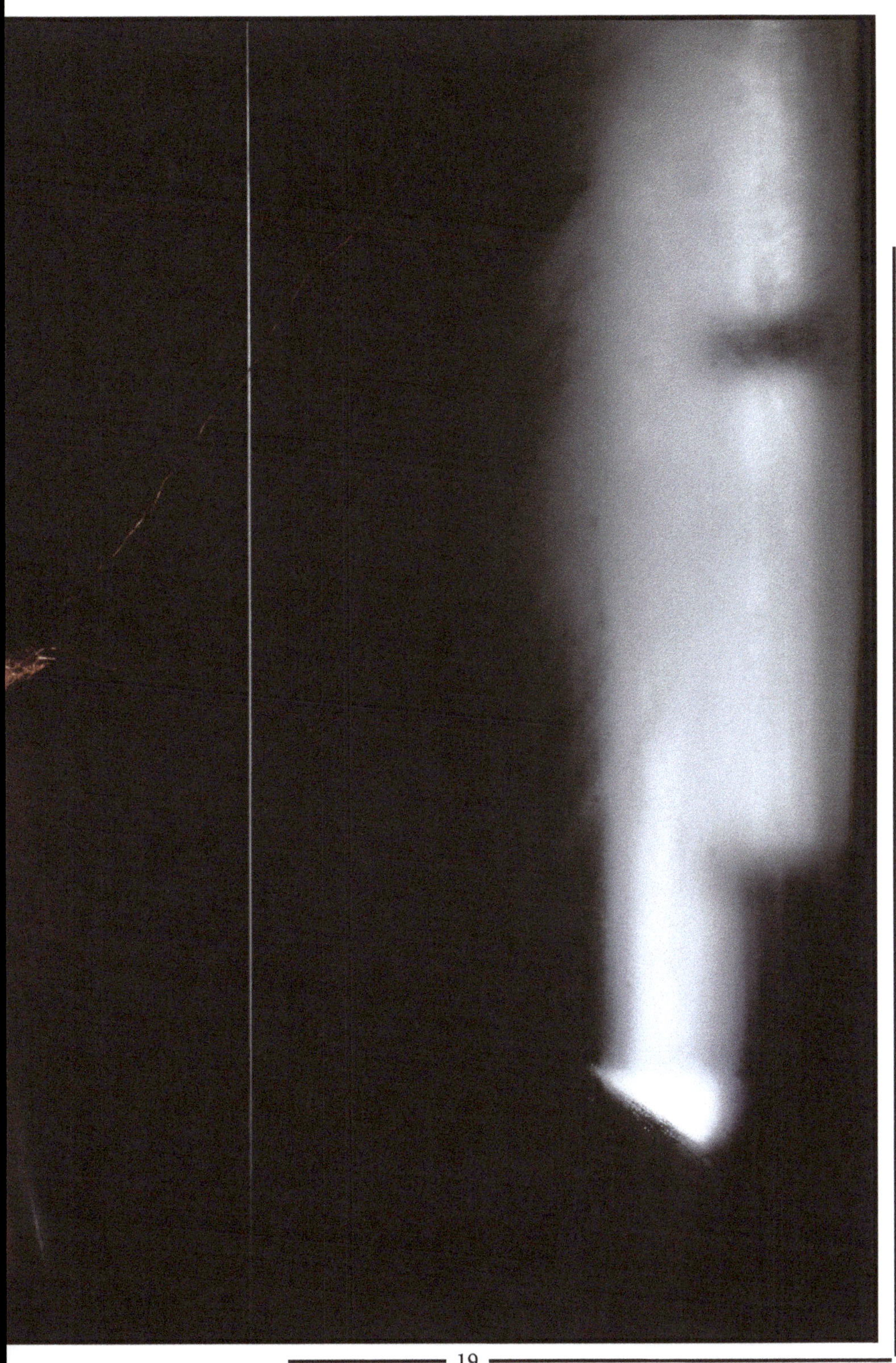

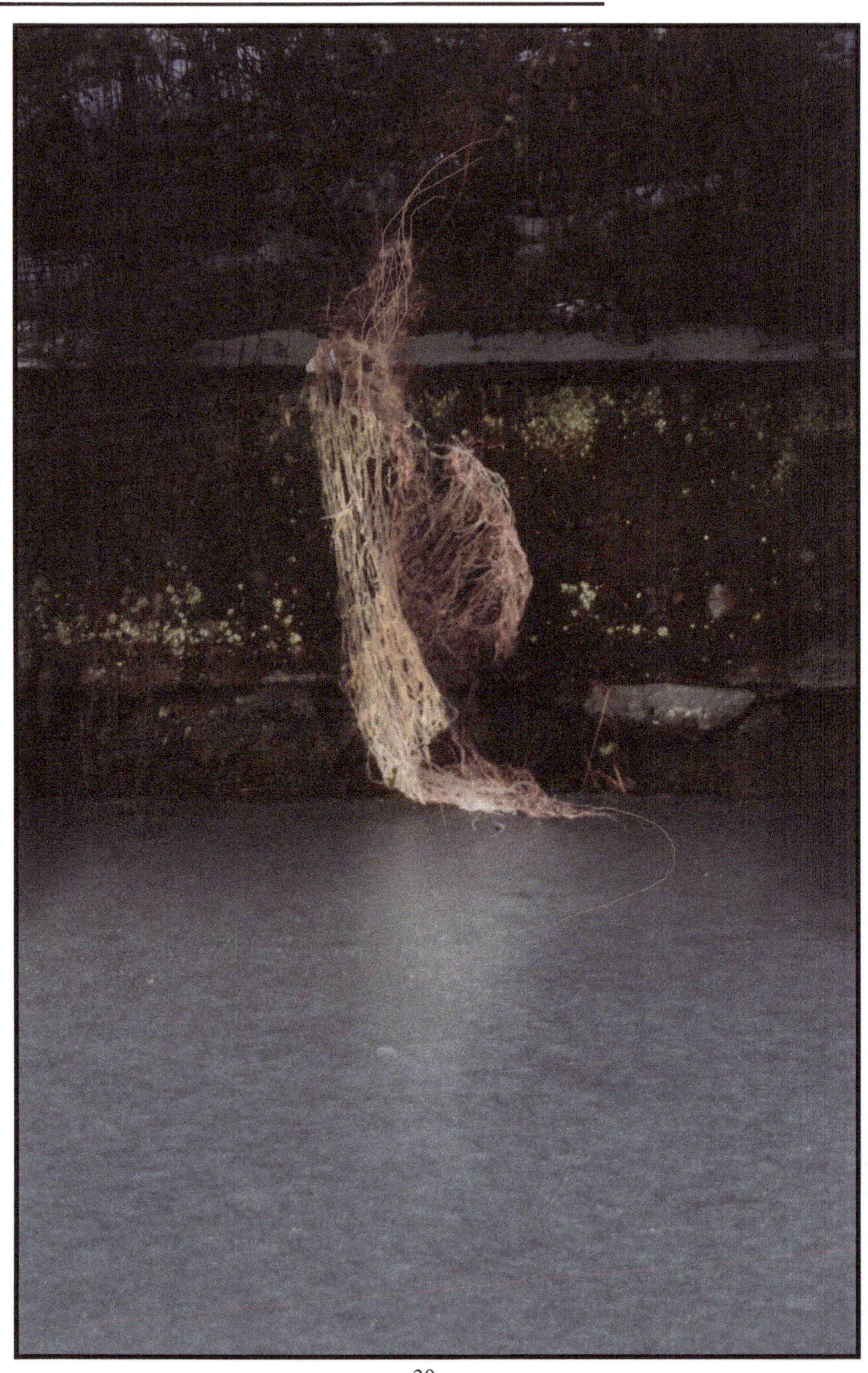

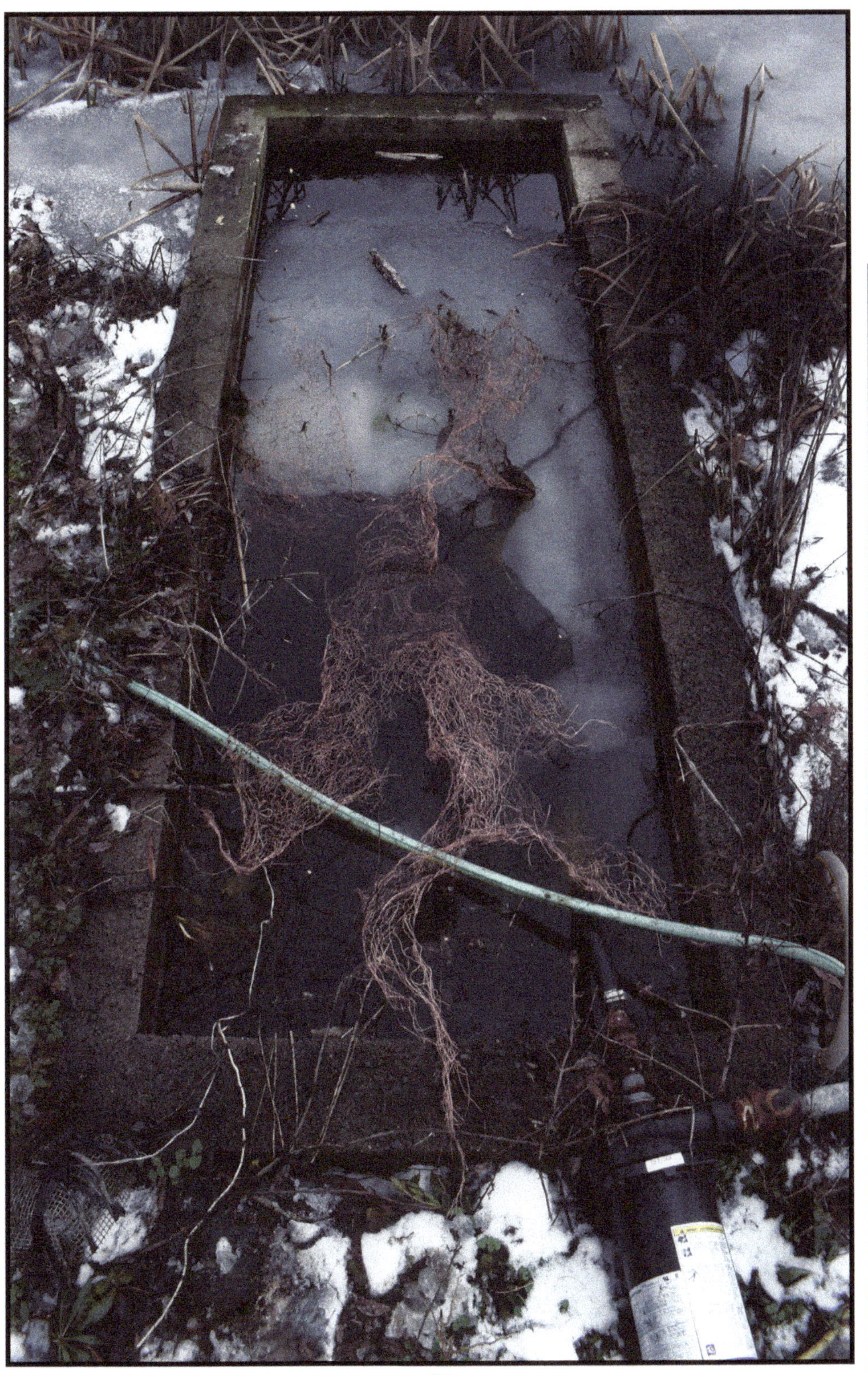

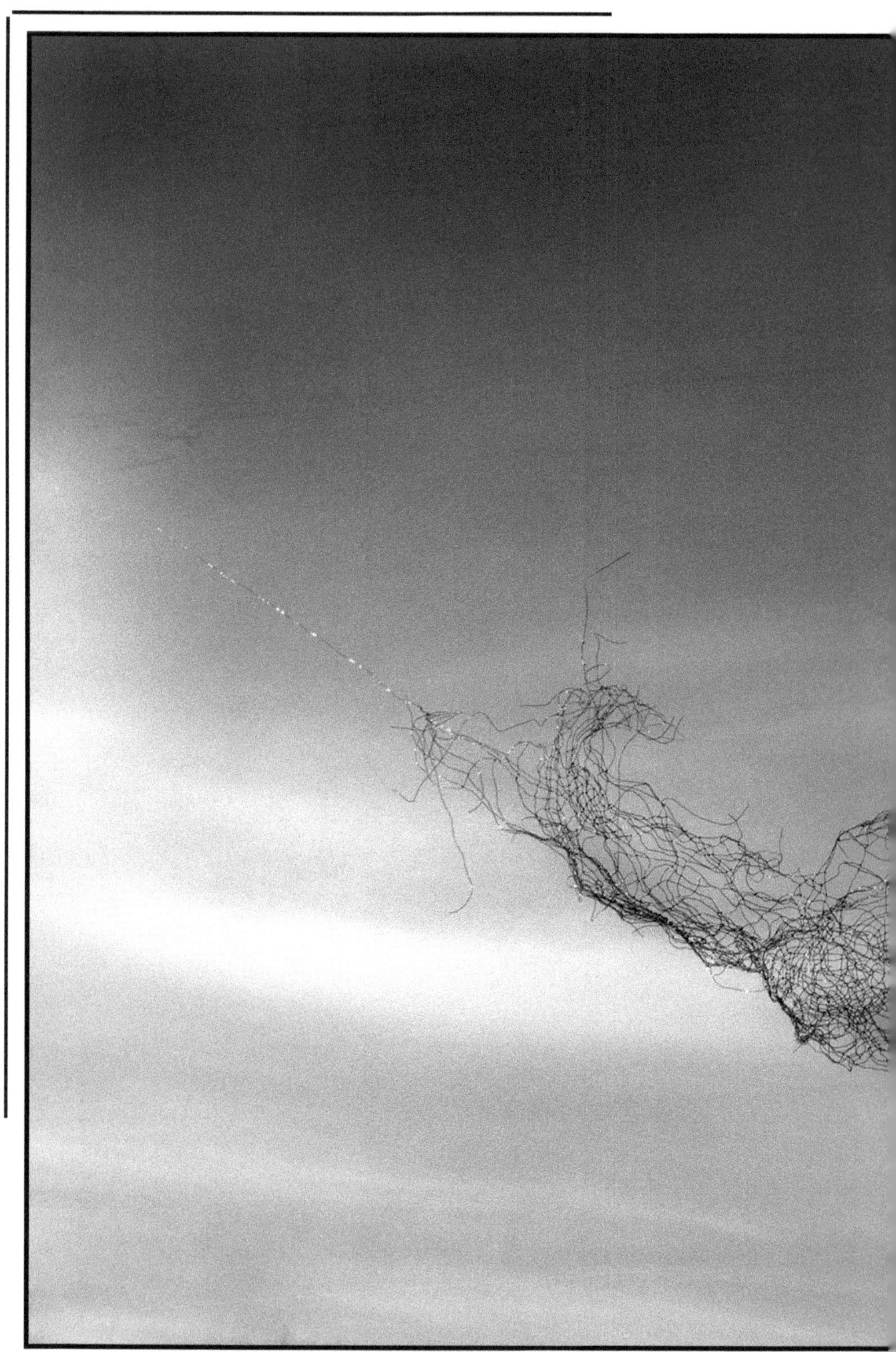

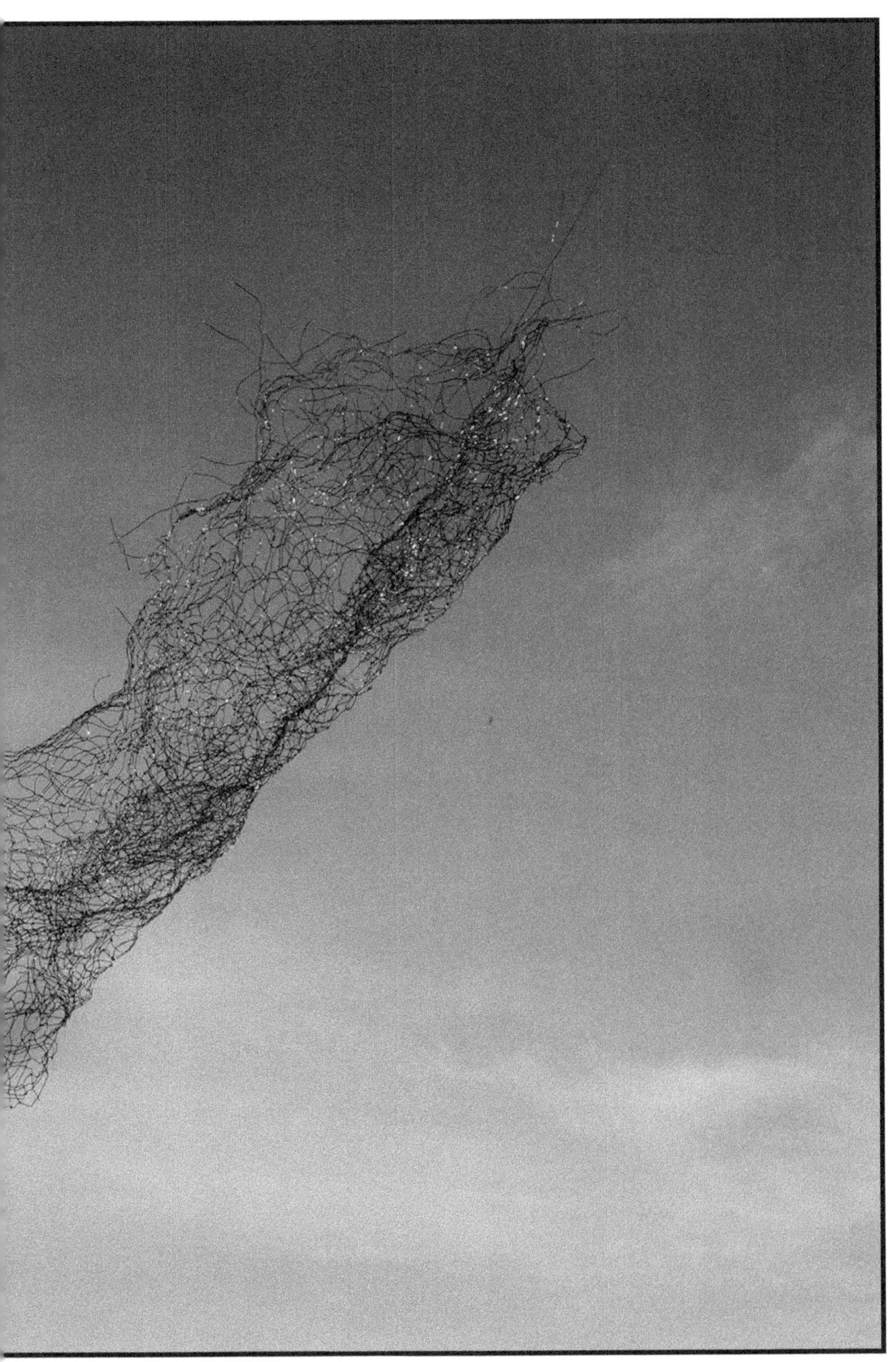

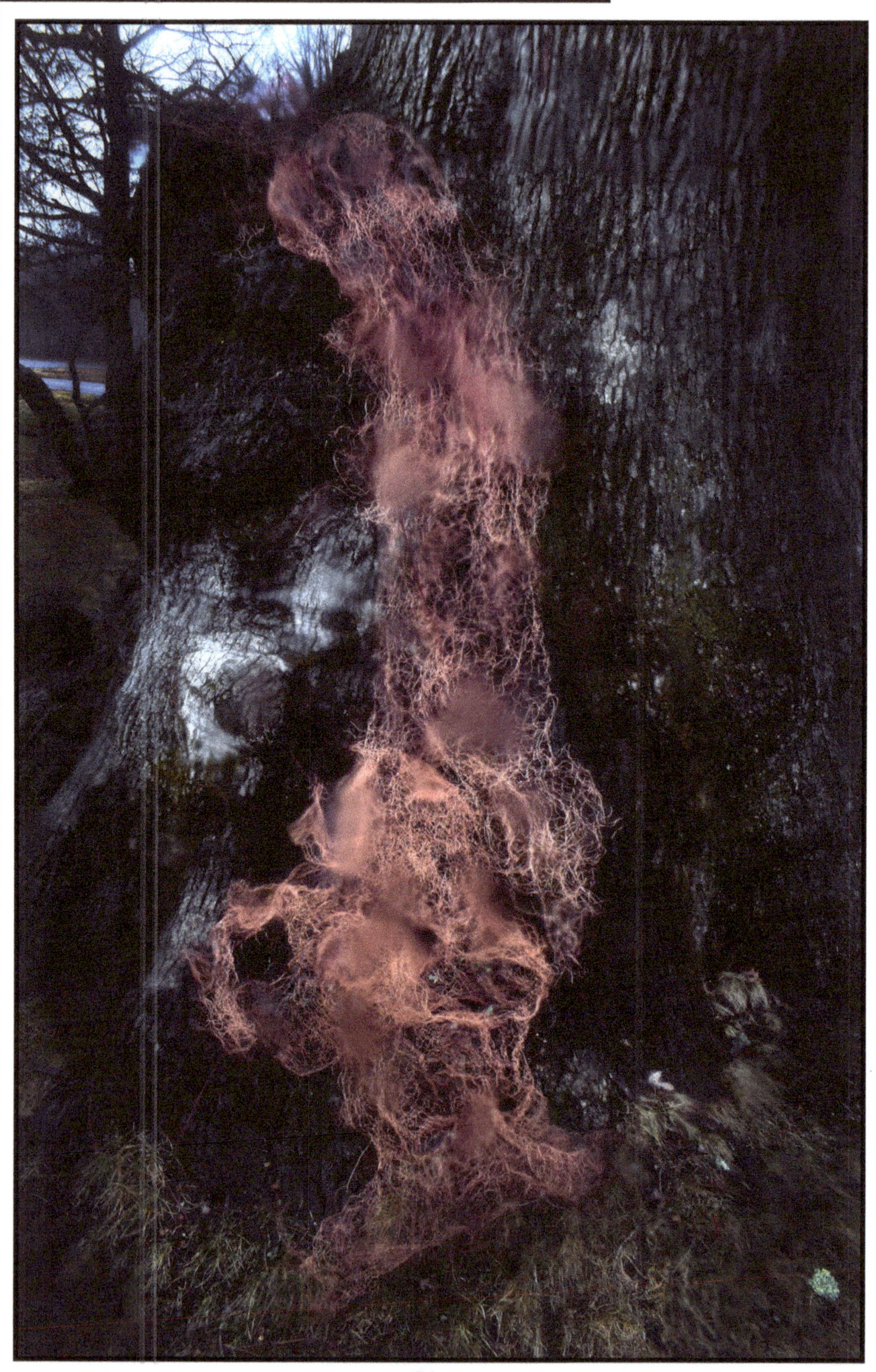

Moonbroch

John Leonard

The safe approach—three laps around a warehouse
where they once filmed *T.V.*

The way darkness stumbles at two in the morning,
winded by the effort, almost like a silent memory.

I took a shovel with me and dug myself a valley.
But death is not a shadow,

nor is it all that evil. And you don't find it in a valley,
unless that valley fills too quickly with snow,

or you're hunted through it by a man with a rifle,
or you sprain your ankle and drown under a rock.

Three times and still not at the point.
What is all this dullness?

I take a step back and find myself near a train yard.

Neon-blackness, like the glow of rain soaked coal.
Nothing doing, when long ago

we tossed our empty cans and stopped reading the light
between railcars as they limped slowly on by.

What other creature would describe
metal boxes as *limping?*

What other creature would start this walk
with three voices and end with none;

as silent as Mercury reflecting off Pittsburgh steel?
Or so the humidity would have you believe.

And so I step forward, with dirt on my hands,
once again into a valley.

Five Days After Your Death

Emily Shoff

For Shandy

Five days after your death, it started to rain. I had been wearing your death like a straightjacket, like a fishskin painted into my own, and everywhere I went, it clung to me.

"I can't get a good breath," I kept saying, though privately I was a little embarrassed. After all, you weren't my own—you weren't my child, my partner. Weren't my parent, my sibling, my friend. Just a student, a graduate from the year before. And yet, your death pierced me.

For close to a year, you'd locked horns with death, but the cancer had pronounced you victor, letting you believe, letting us all believe you were okay. Then nine months later, it snuck back in and gored you when your back was turned.

I thought I knew unfair, thought I was prepared for it. I'd lived for close to forty-four years, read the books—taught them for God's sake—seen plenty of it up-close in my small town: the fathers ripped down by avalanches, the mothers toppled by cancer, bad news ricocheting off the box canyon walls like dynamite, the smoke hovering for days before dissipating and joining the atmosphere where pain lives.

But this—to say it was unfair was like burning half your body and calling it hot. This felt cruel in a way I'd only before ascribed to violence. You had things to do. The obvious—the years in college, the cute boyfriend who didn't matter, the summer frolicking in Europe...

But there were other things, thousands of things, things you didn't know, couldn't know: The birth of a child, the heat of her small body against yours, the sound of "Momma" when it is called out across a crowd, the patter of those same feet running towards you and up into your arms, her head leaning into yours, the scent of tea and sweat and the soap you'd bathed her in rising...

All those, you would miss. All those, I had had. This, too, tugged at my skin, stretching it, ripping it. All the days when I'd been angry and petty and mean, when I'd said fine, if this is it, I don't want it. I thought I'd be more, that I'd mean more. How small I'd been in my quest for big.

It rained all night and into the morning and when at last it lifted, the world remained quiet, the birds stunned into silence, the clouds heavy. Until, finally, from across the woods, a lone bluebird called out, its song like a flute rippling out at the start of a symphony. I imagined its violet blue throat pulsing with the thrill of living, with the hope for love. Its entire body must have gone into that song, so bright and piercing was each note, backed by the rush of air. Then it, too, fell quiet, and the rain settled back in.

I Name This Scar My Brother

Terence Degnan

I call the house we tried to topple
Jericho

the cotton between the arguments
I call *The Holy Ghost*

we *modified our Saharas*
by the grass stains in our jeans

every crawdad
was a kraken

every home we turned our backs on
eventually became salt

my old man used to wear a serpent
to hold his pants in place

every birthday was a Pentecost
every pencil held a pentagram

every deep-end seemed to magnify
the angles of our animals

when God was just a dog ear
in the epilogue

or a curfew that escapes
when the window breaks

a forgotten knot on a bed sheet
like scattered beads

between the car seats
from a broken dashboard rosary

we were told sainthood
required three miracles

so we rode our bikes
with our arms crossed like pharaohs

across our concave chests
we puffed them out like roosters

as we passed our annual
roman candle tests

we changed out of our uniforms
into altar robes

in the gauntlets of the rectories
squeaking past the minotaurs

where, in the land of children
the one-eyed priest was king

I name this wound, my brother
the one he couldn't shield

from the stubbled hour he spent
dozing beneath the fabled tree

to the year he began to shave
in the era of hollowed-out bibles

when magazines hid
in magazines

every sibling has a gap in his childhood
every sapling

an emergent tooth
on the timberline

there are miracles you have to perform
without gods

days you have to escape
by ignorance

sometimes a rite of passage
aligns with another's viaticum

sometimes what you thought was water
isn't water

when your brother
hands you a flask

and says, *here*
drink this

Cardinal Sins

Moises Ramos

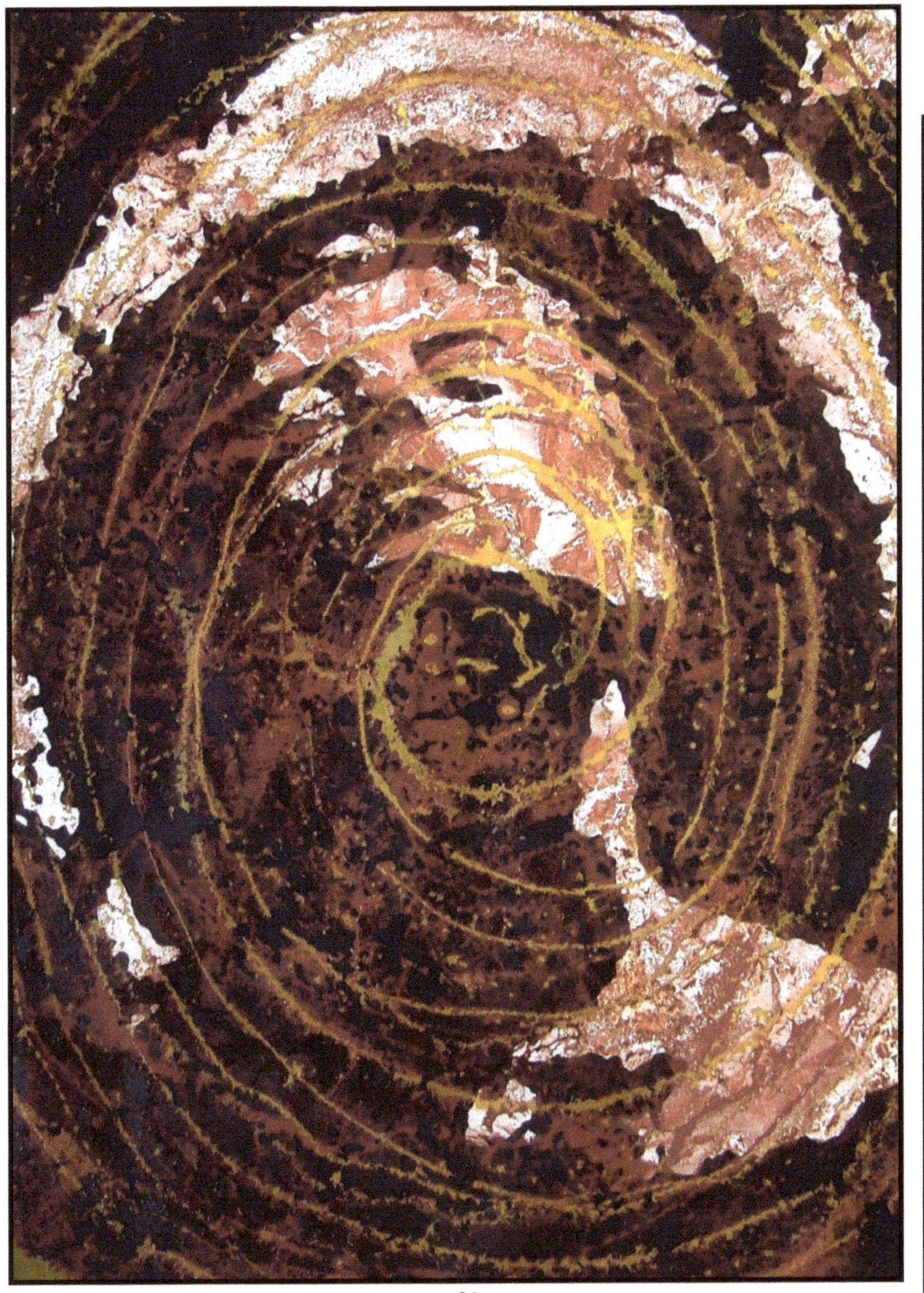

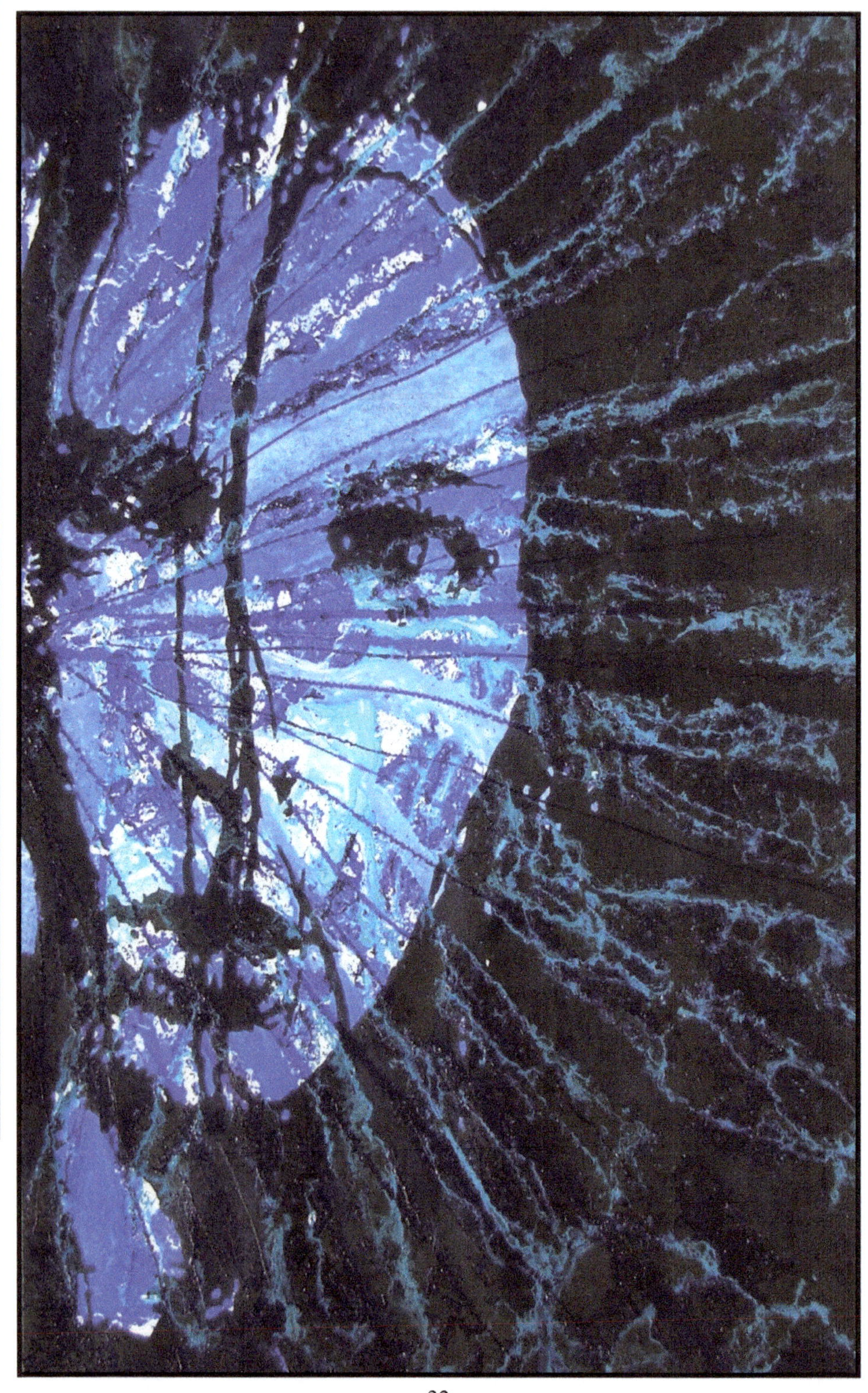

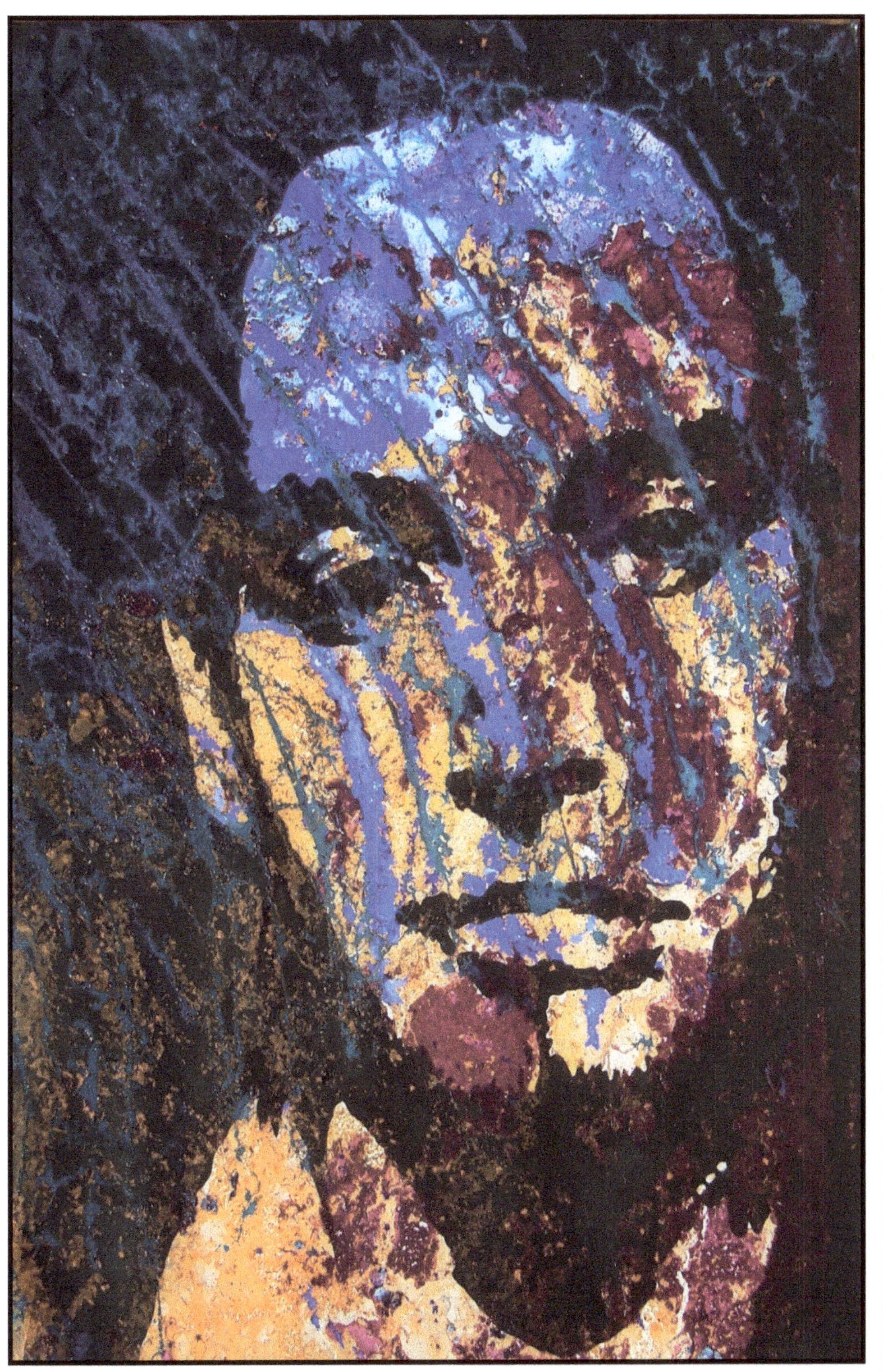

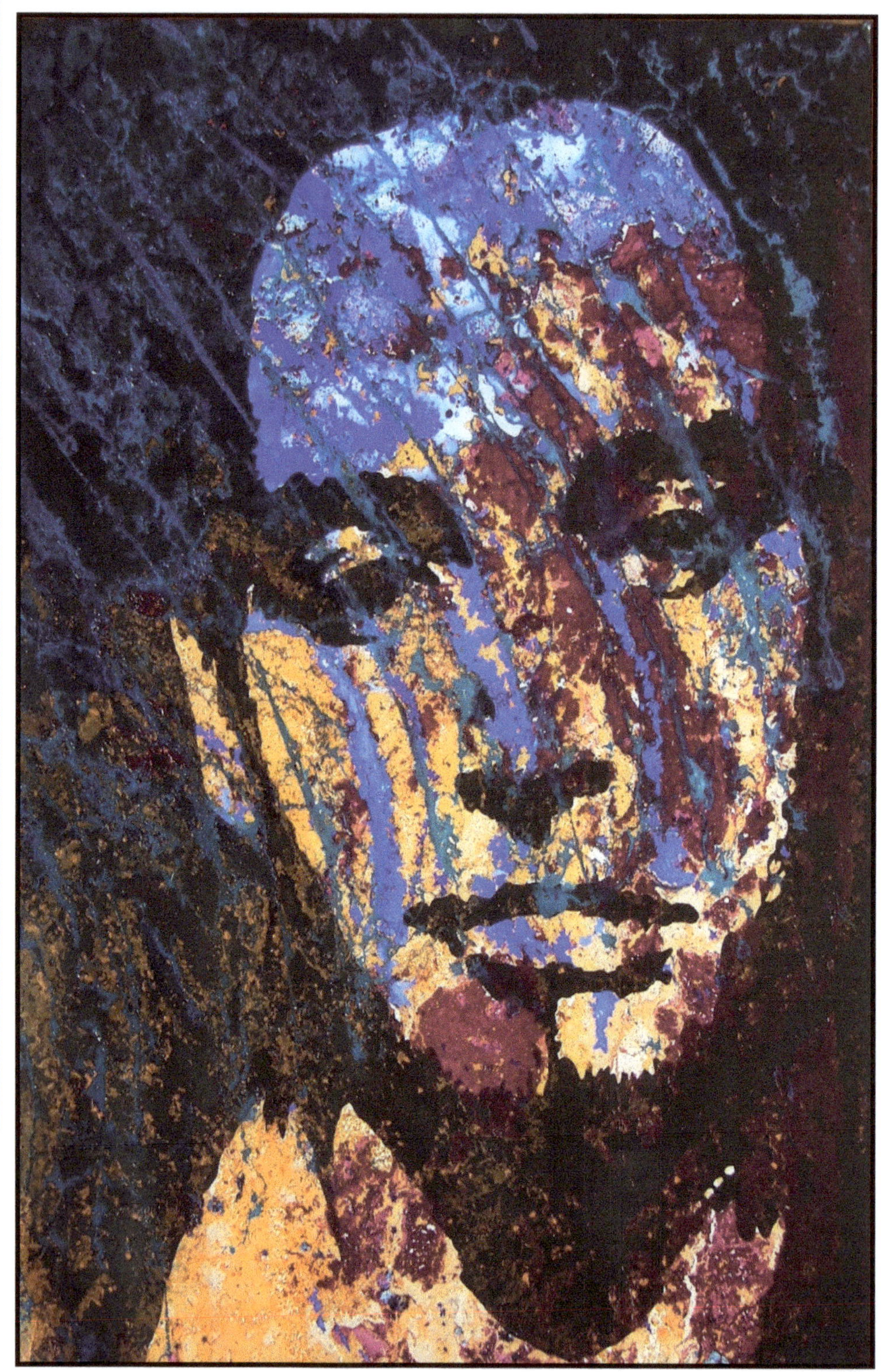

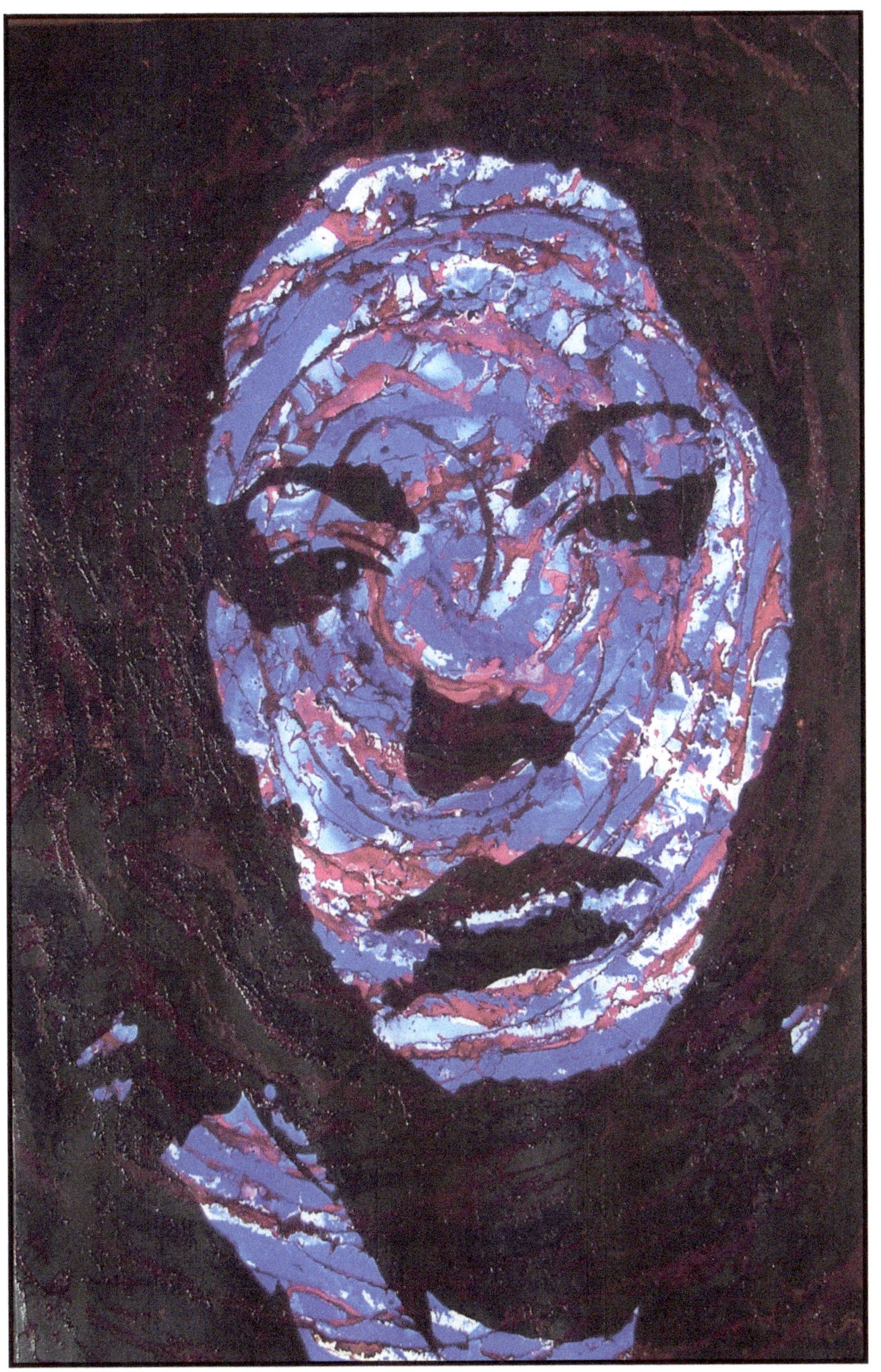

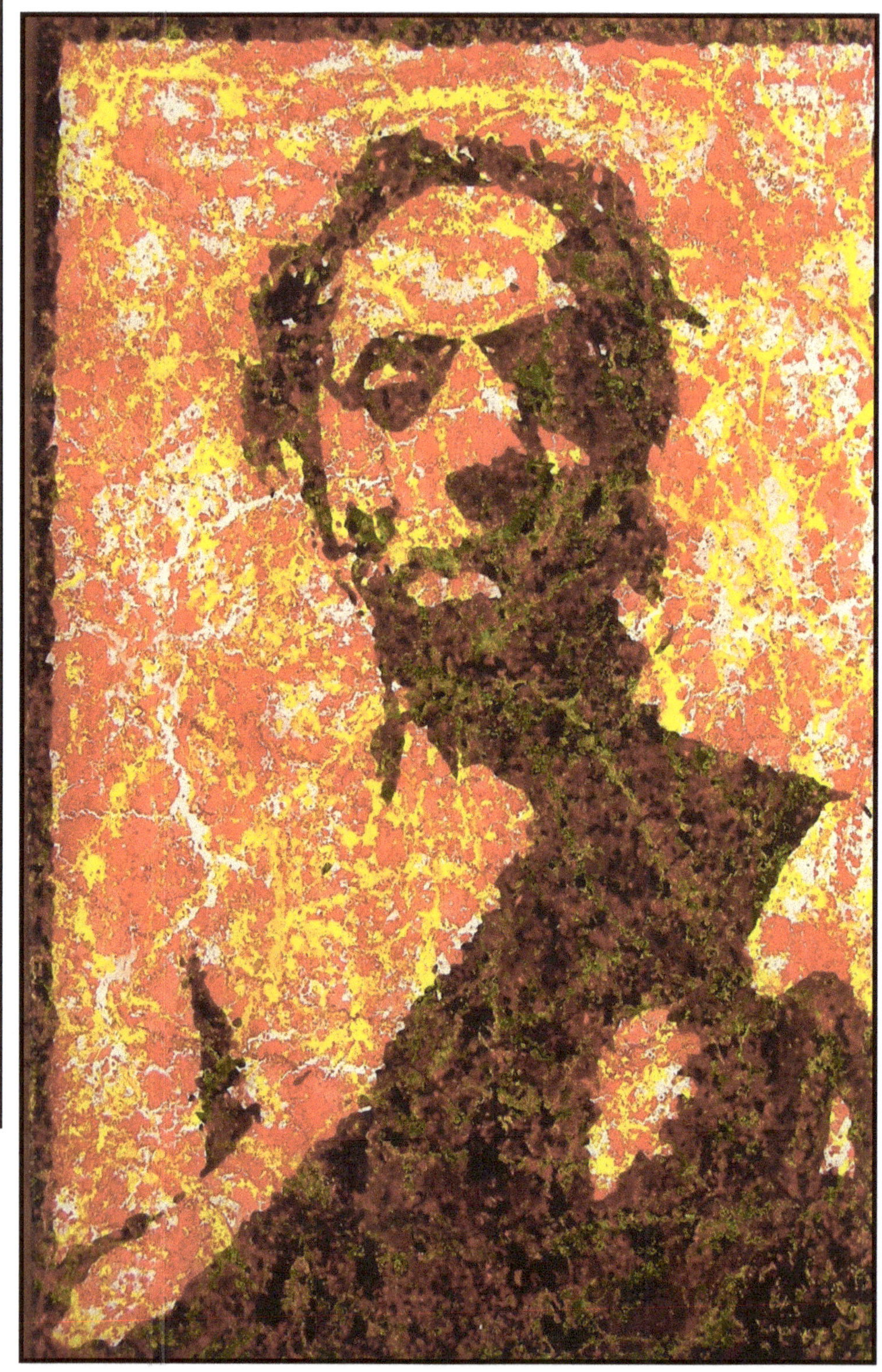

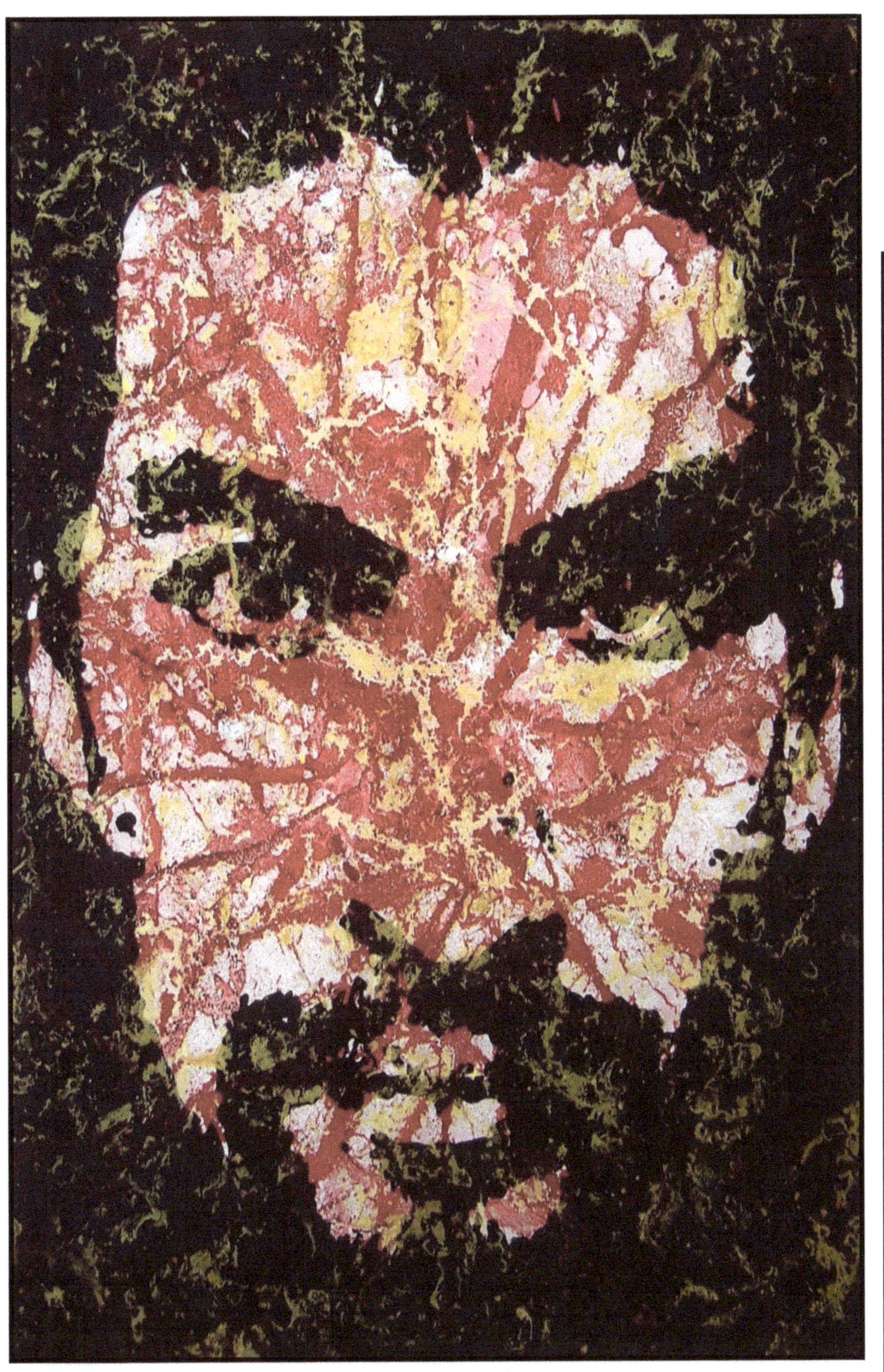

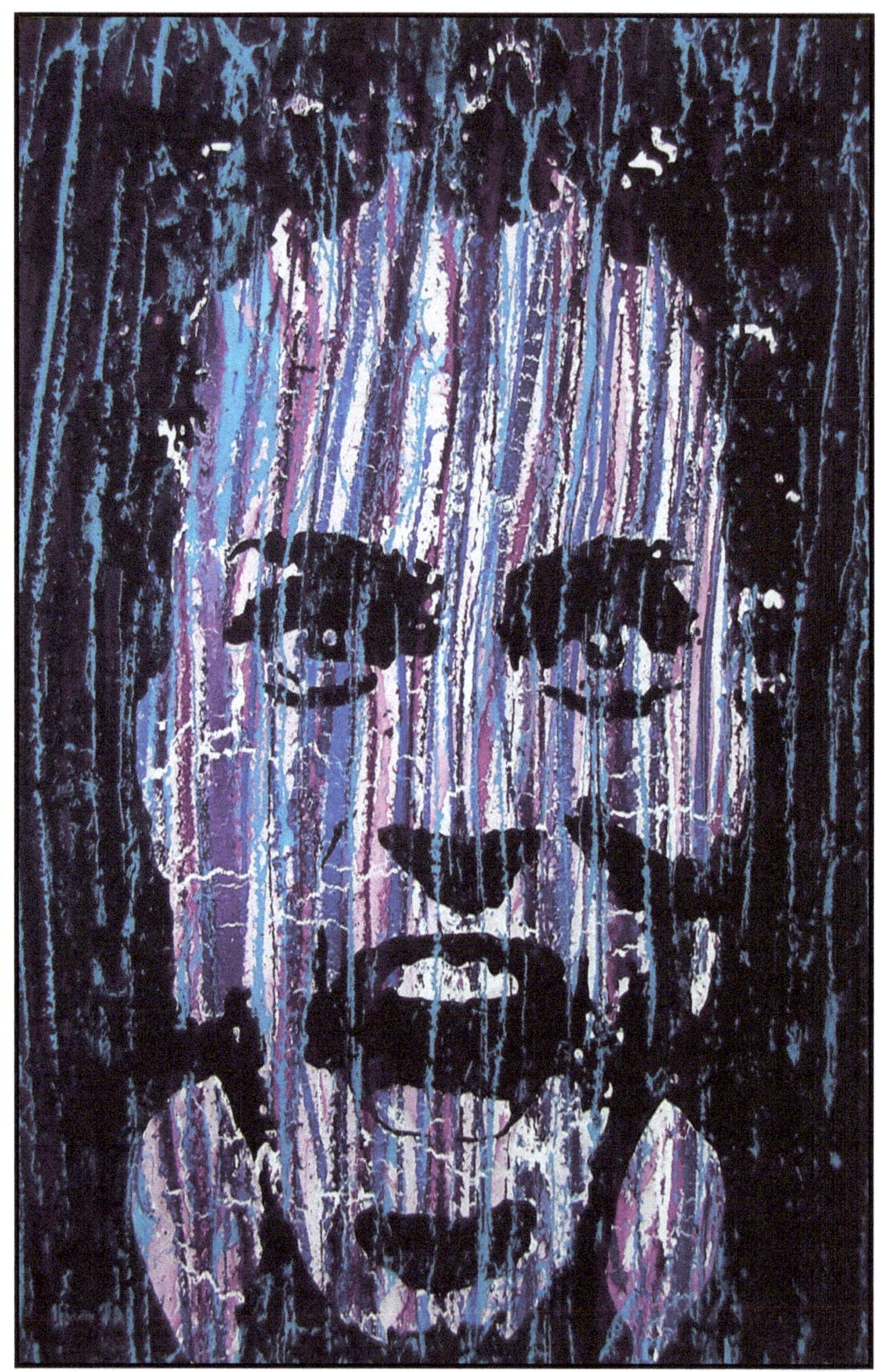

Surprise

Kate MacDonald

I'm not worried about leaving,
as in "Death where is thy sting"
but the manner of my passing,
now that's a different thing.

There are certain ways of going
that I really wouldn't mind,
with stories told at gatherings
by those I've left behind.

I don't want to be hang gliding
if anything goes awry,
screaming the name of every deity
as I hurtle from the sky.

I would not like to be eating
that exotic Fugu fish,
then thanks to Chef's ineptitude
be found face down in my dish.

After some deliberation
on the form of my demise,
there are too many variations,
let it come as a surprise.

Talks With God

Joanna Acevedo

I talked to God this week. He said, no. He said, spare the rod and spoil the child. He grunted. He smoked a clove cigarette. I am getting used to the fireworks, but the gunshots wake me up at night. I am standing up to the firing squad. If you were an infection, what type would you be? I am seriously considering the guillotine. I am pondering the usefulness of the ball-gag. What is your favorite sort of weapon? Mine is your face, after it rains.

I walk along the edge of a blade, trying to keep my balance. The cuts to my feet are shallow and bleed freely. This is supposedly a metaphor; for what, I'm not sure. When I talked to God, he said we should spend more quality time doing things we like to do, like playing chess or sadomasochism. God has lots of good advice; most of it is lost to the ages. Scripture has very few answers; instead I turn inward. If you were a question, what kind would you be?

Lobotomy

Lino Azevedo

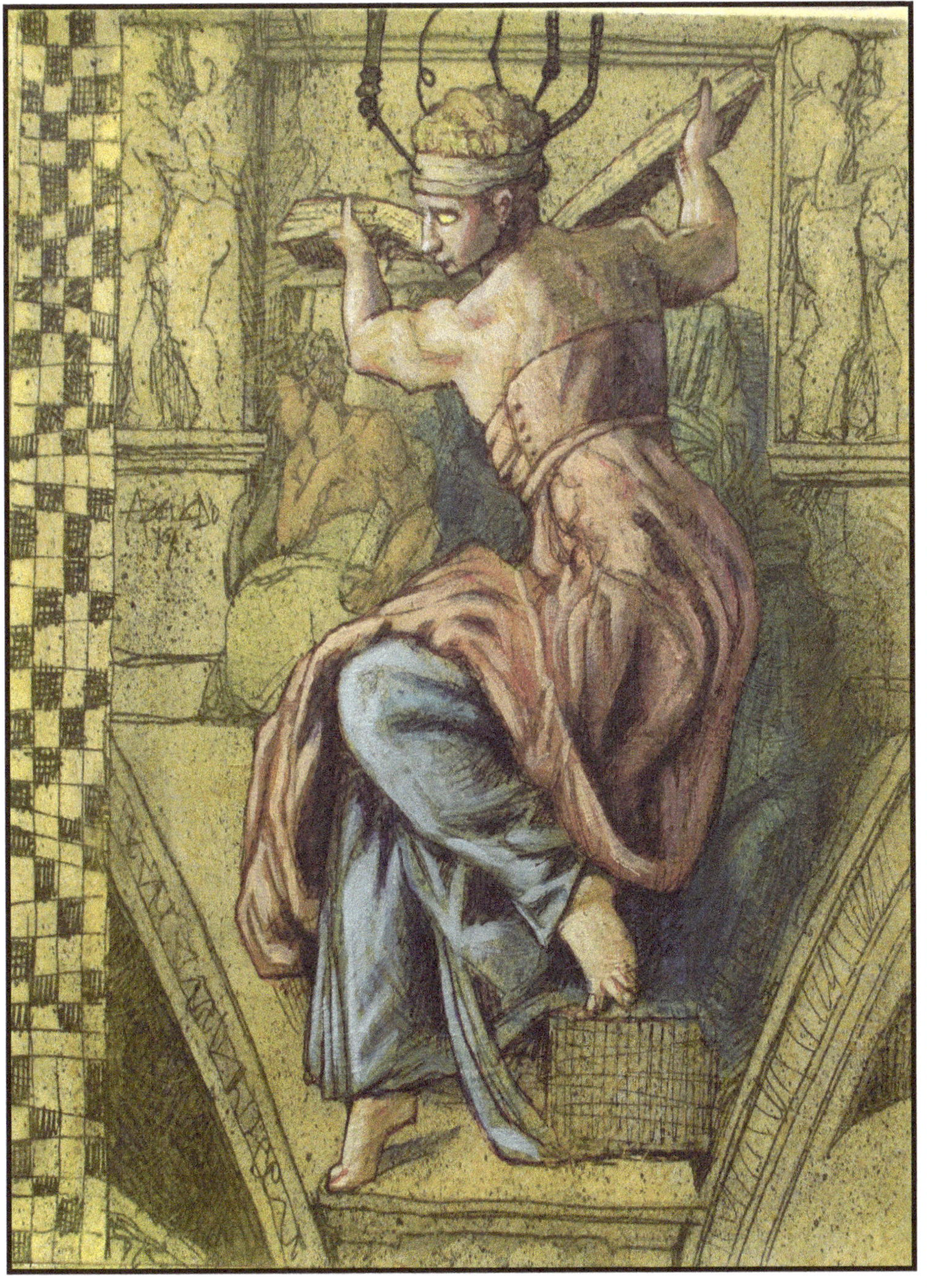

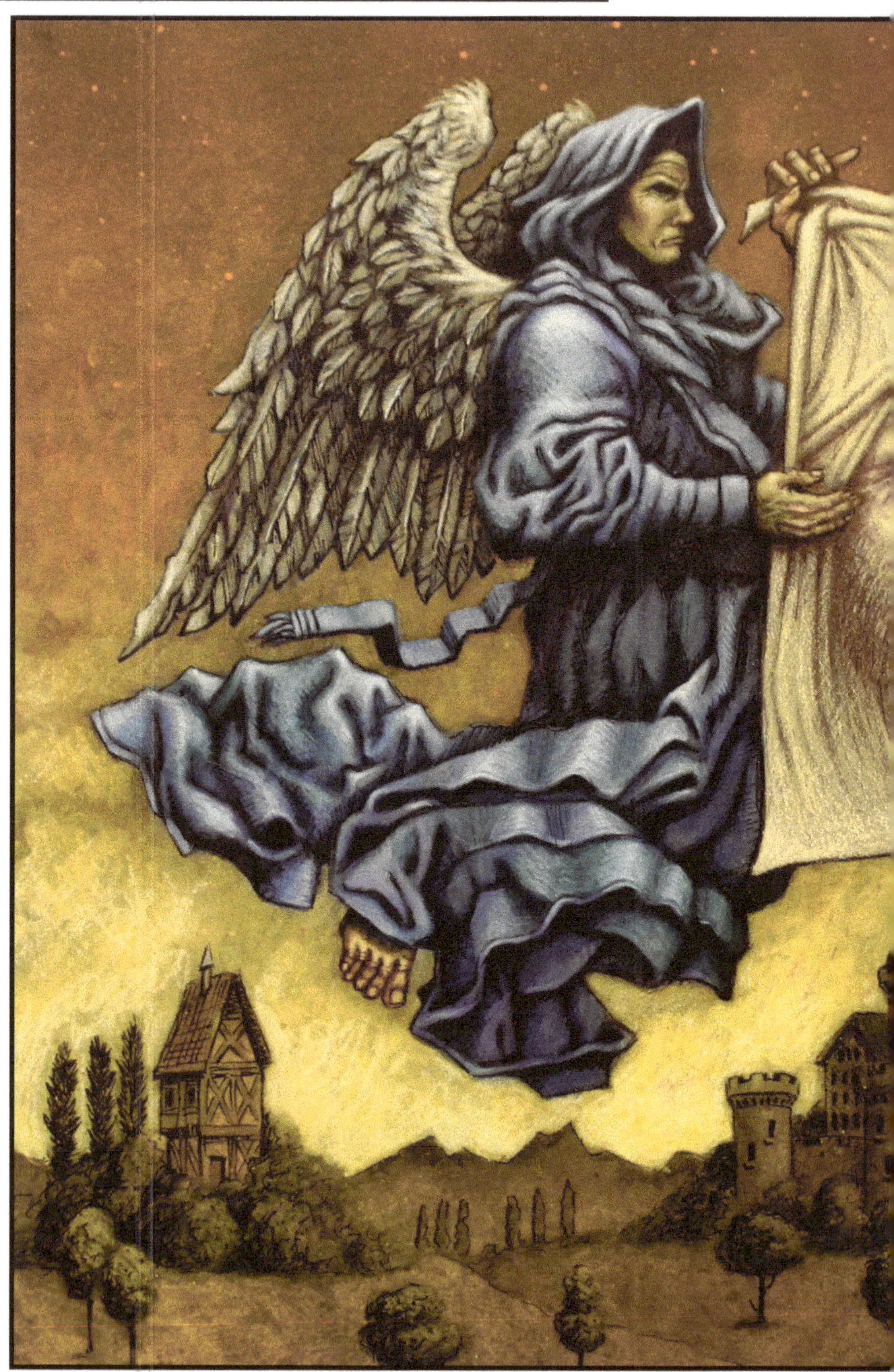

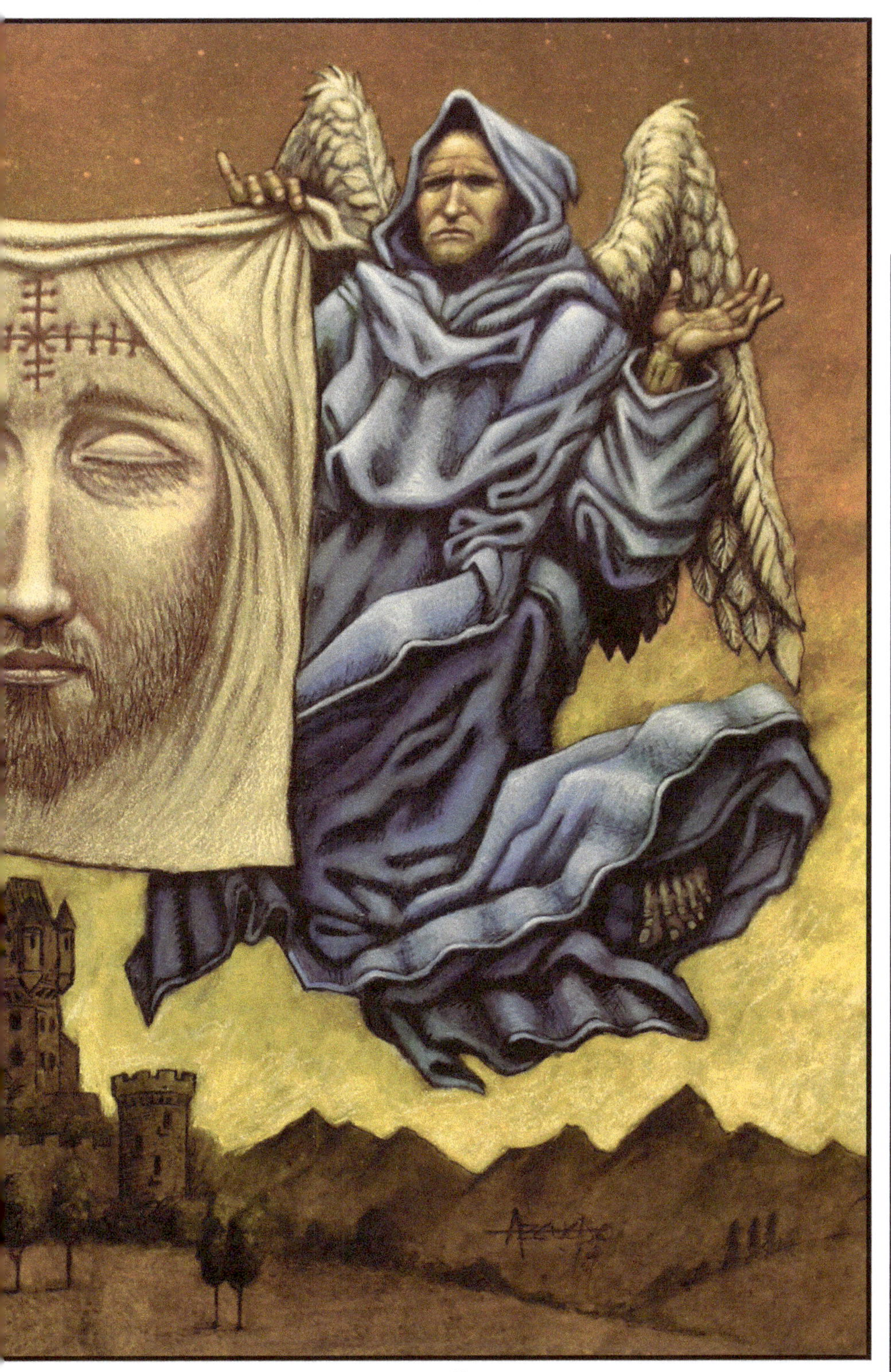

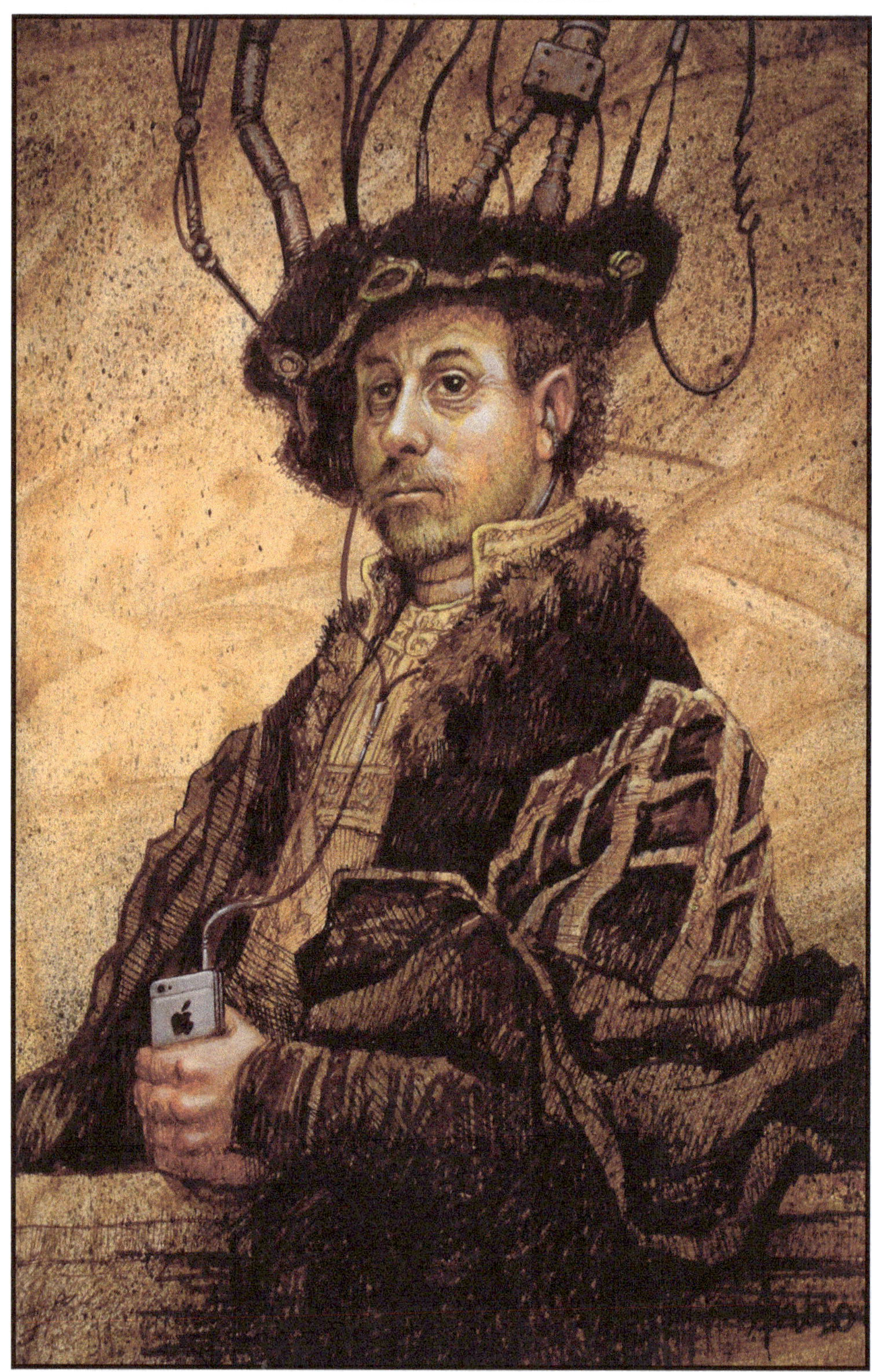

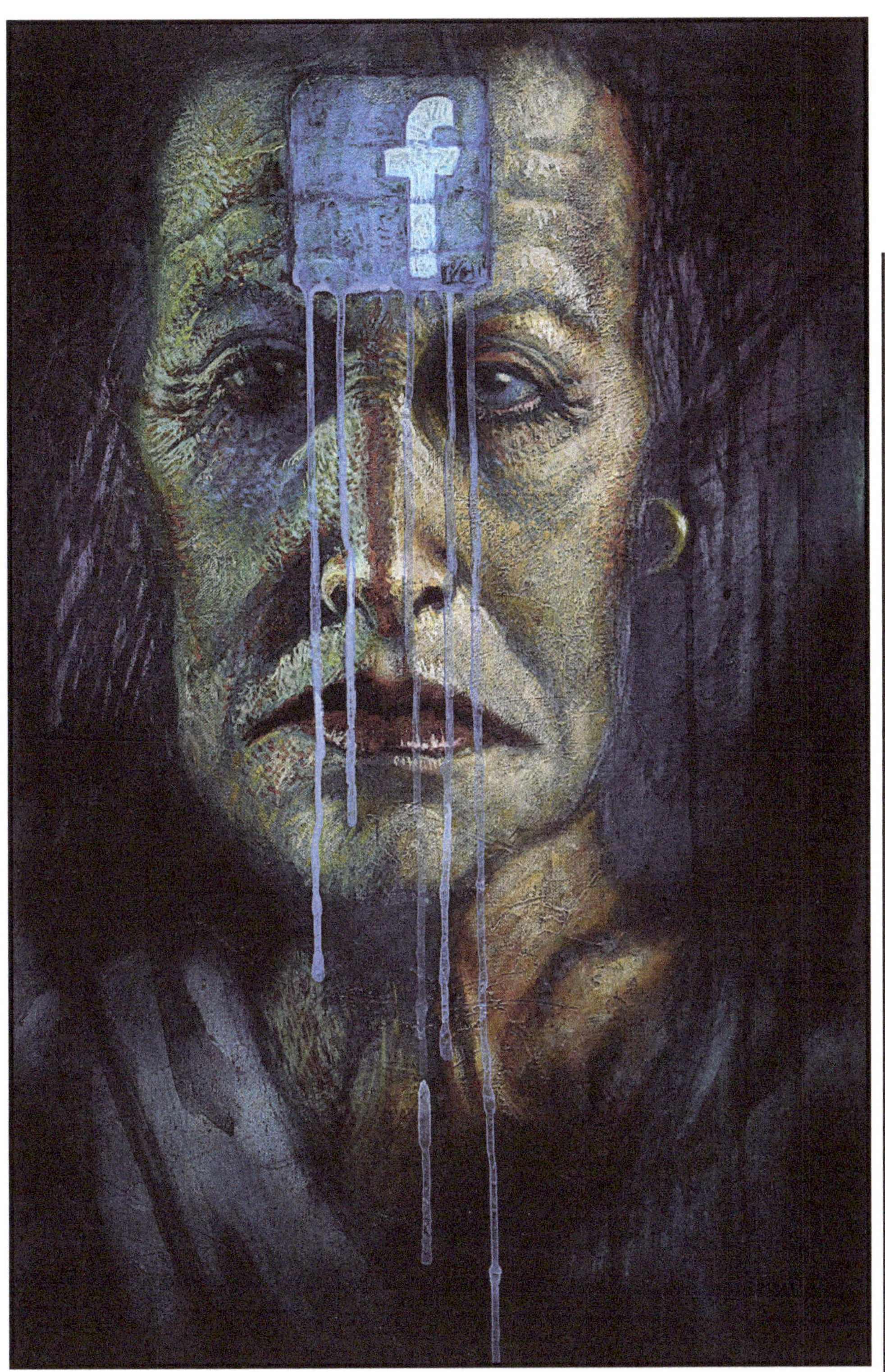

f

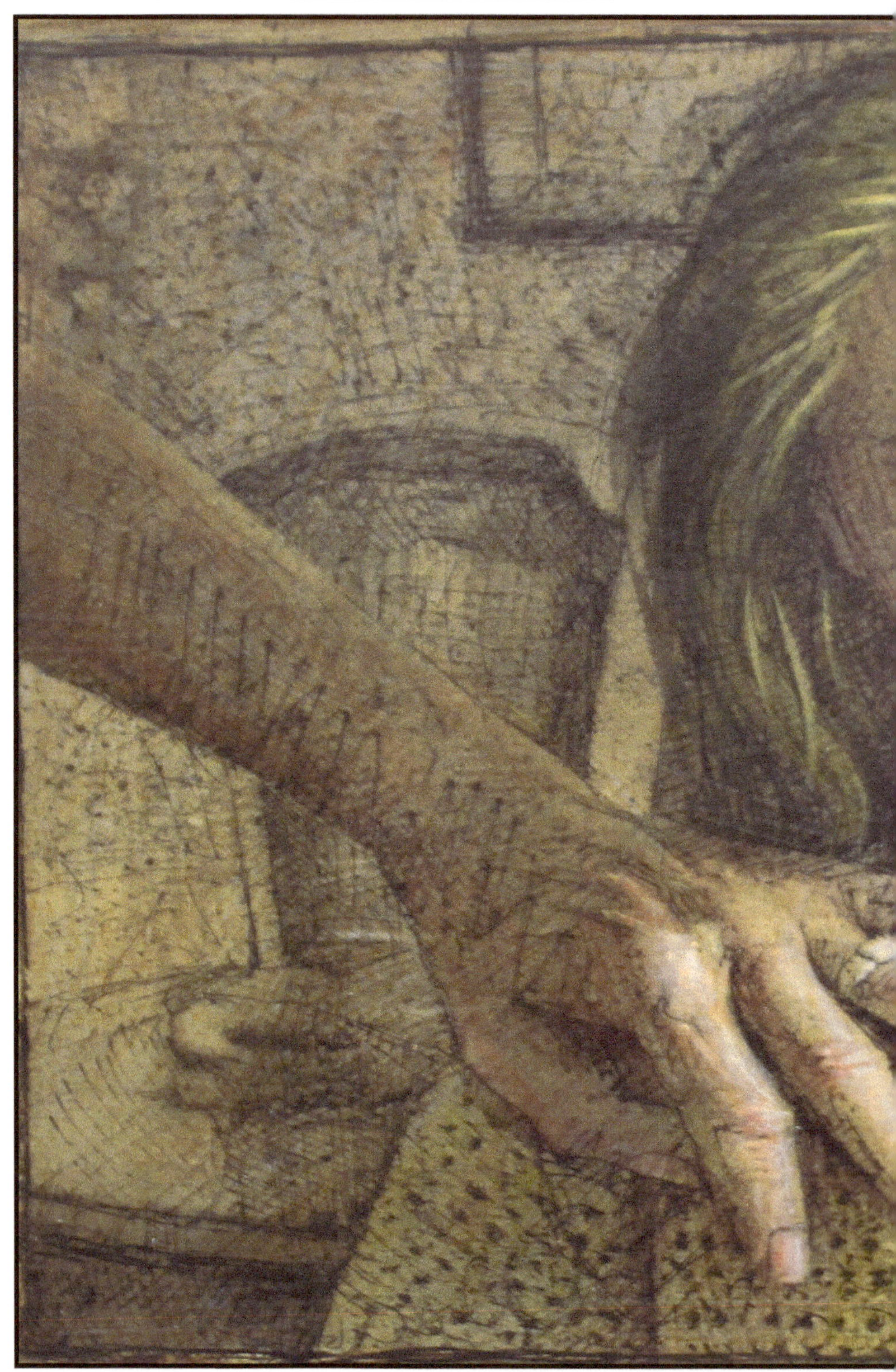

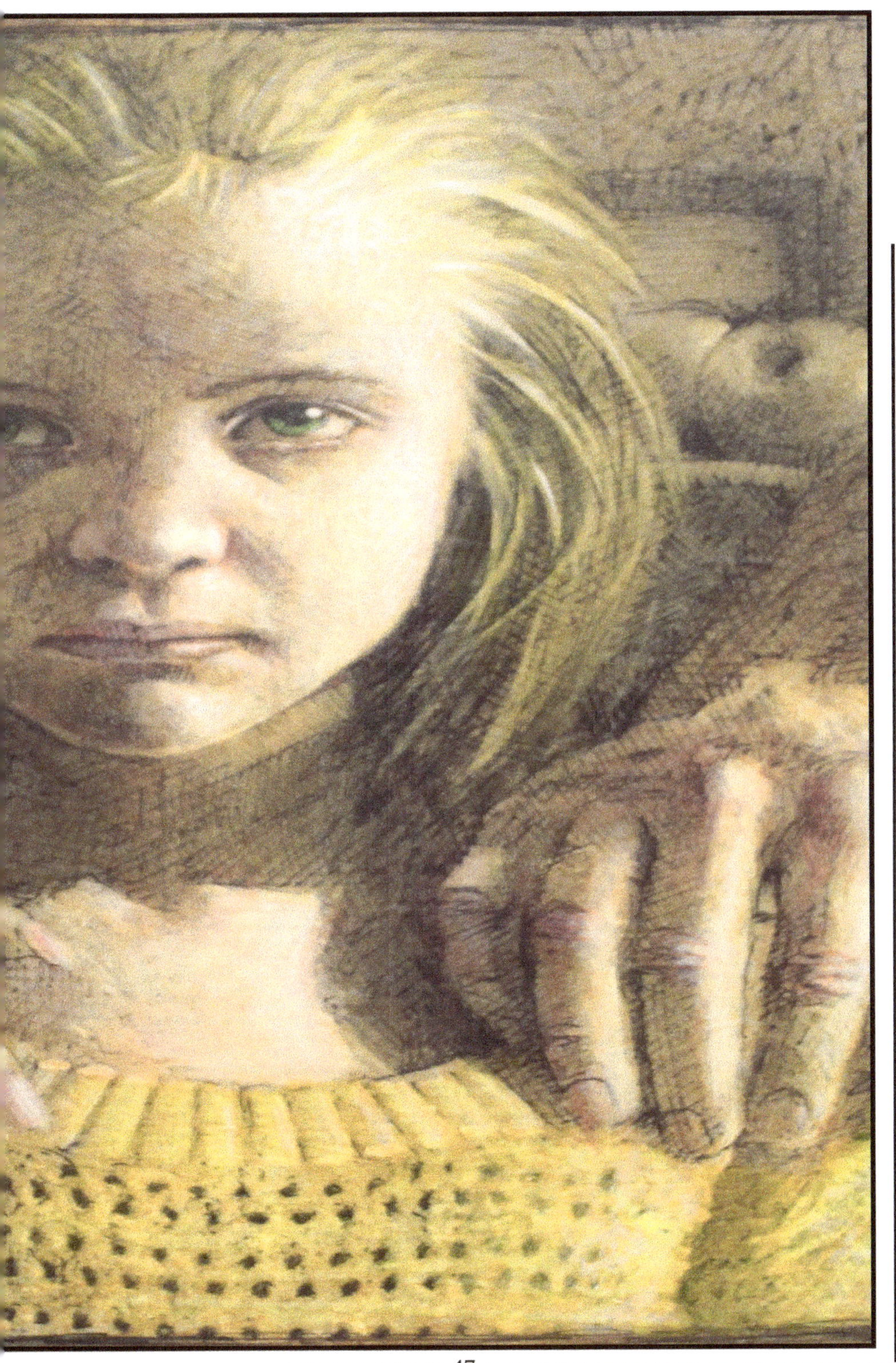

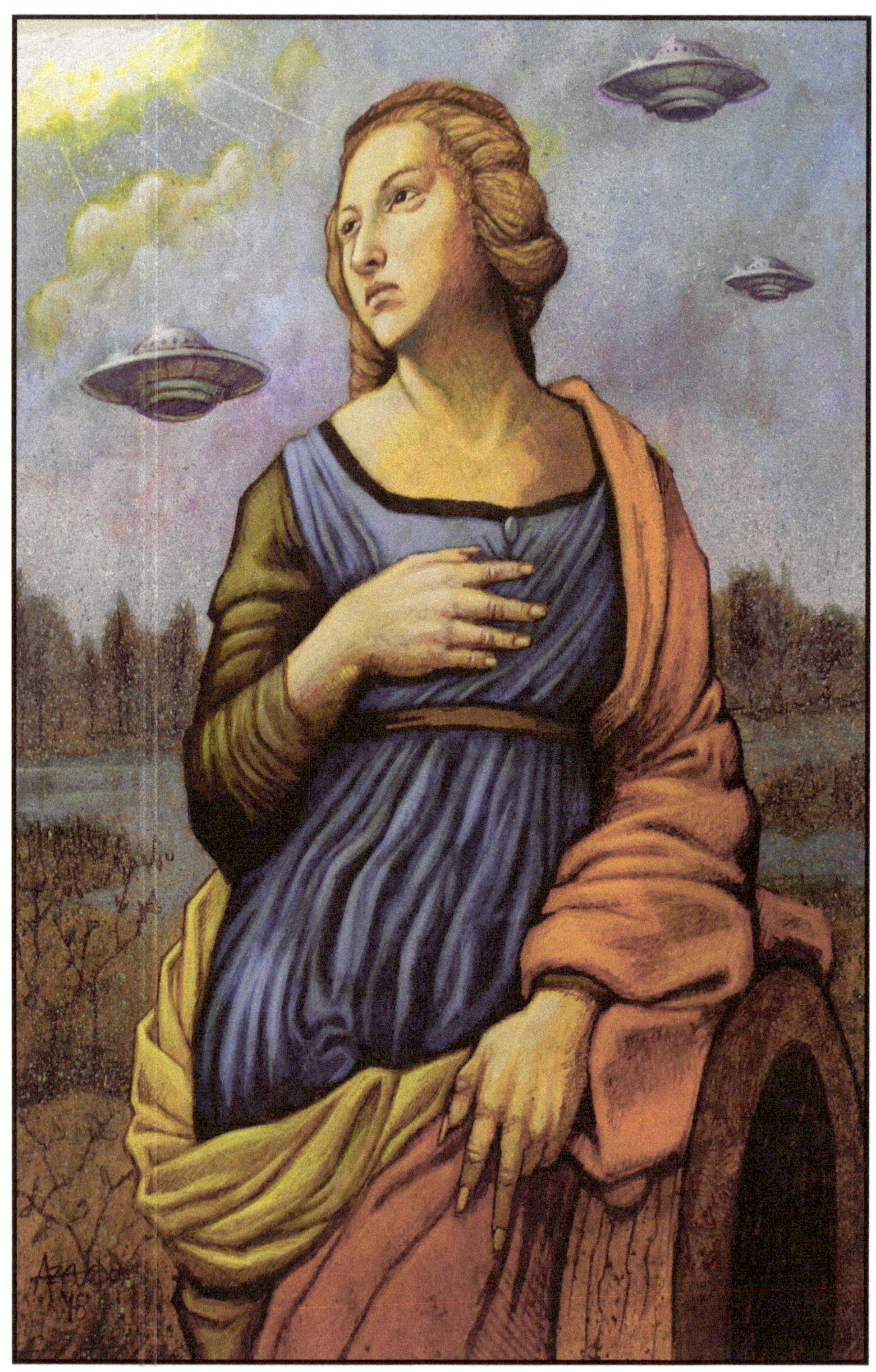

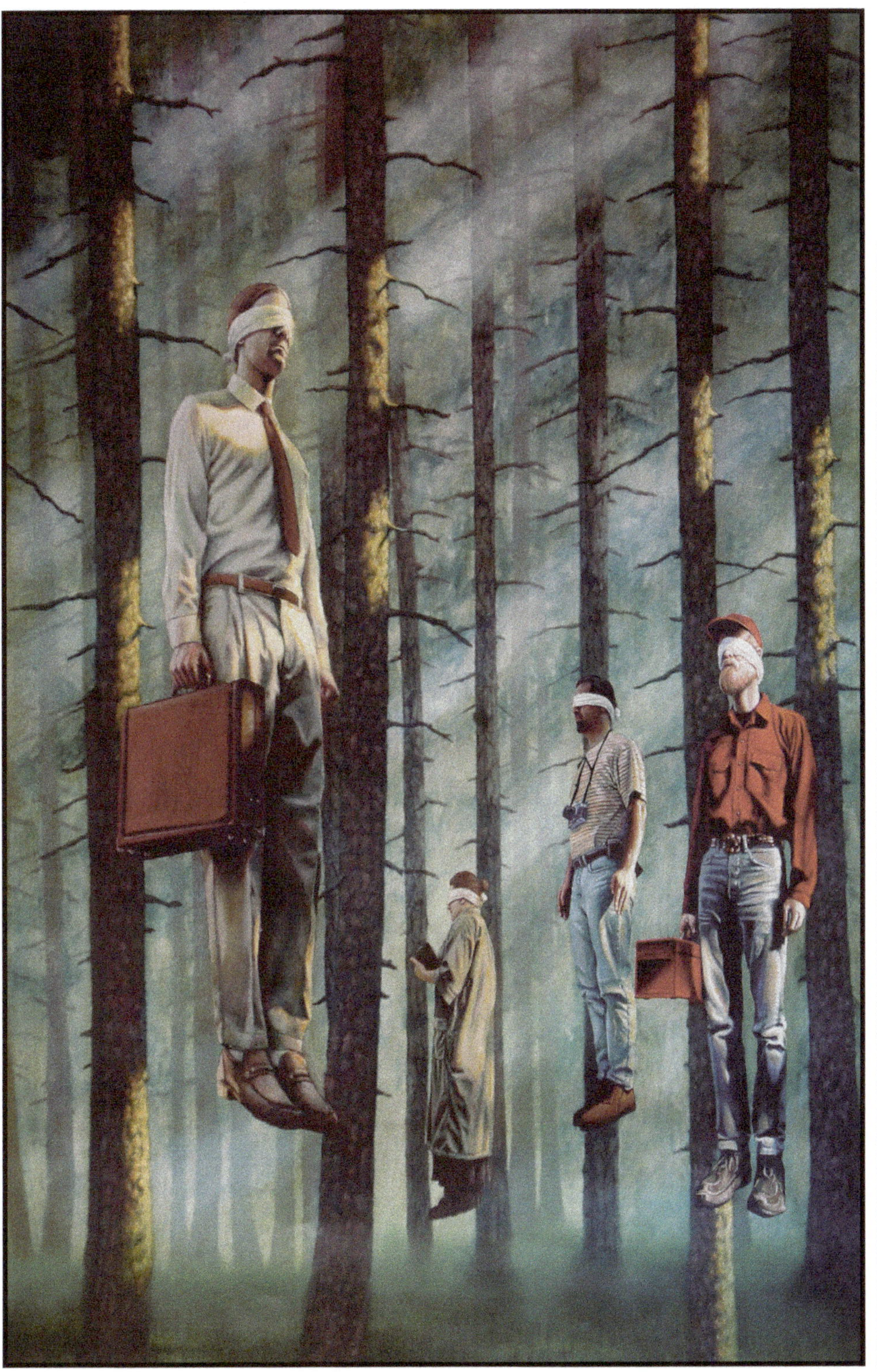

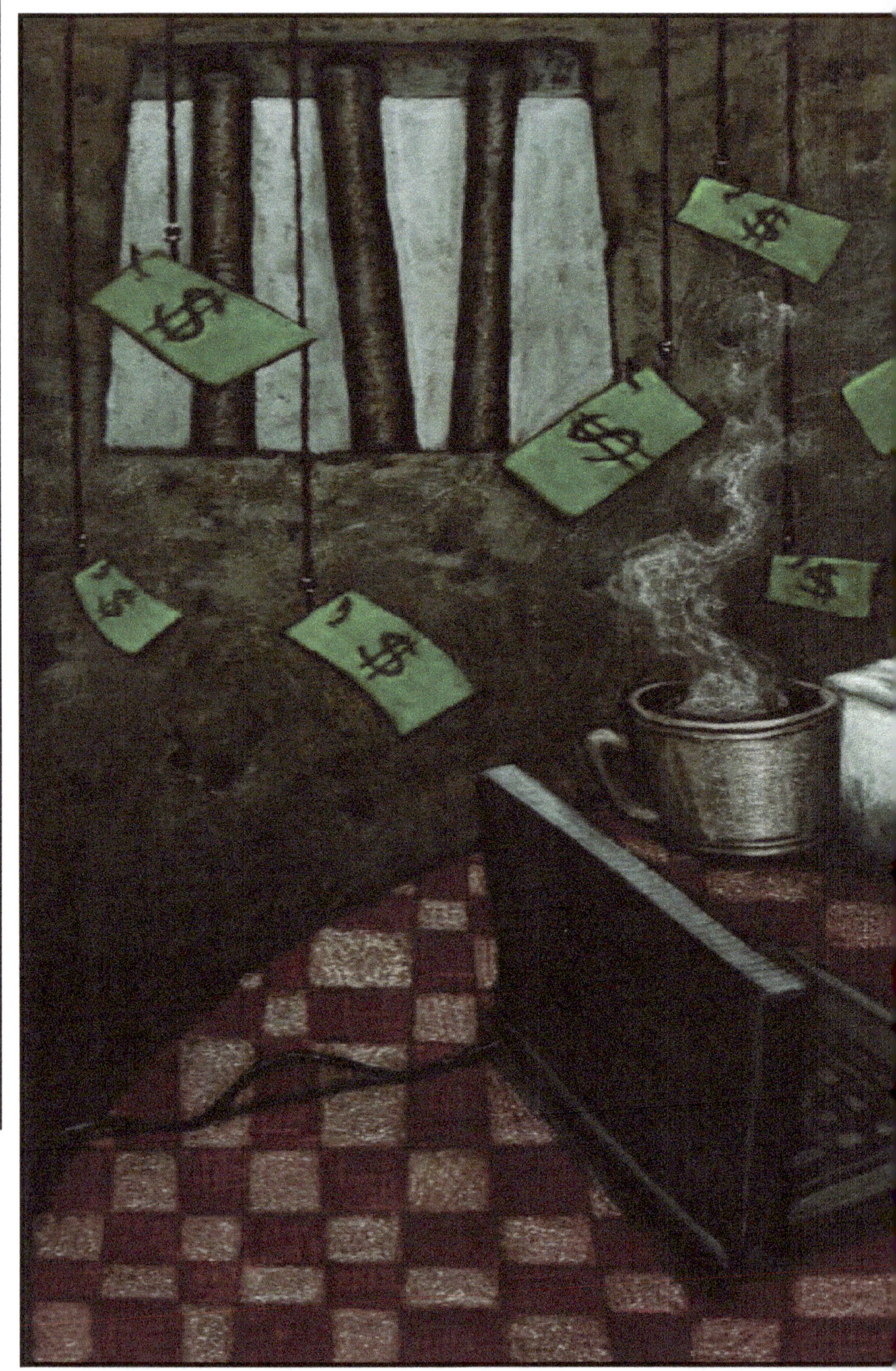

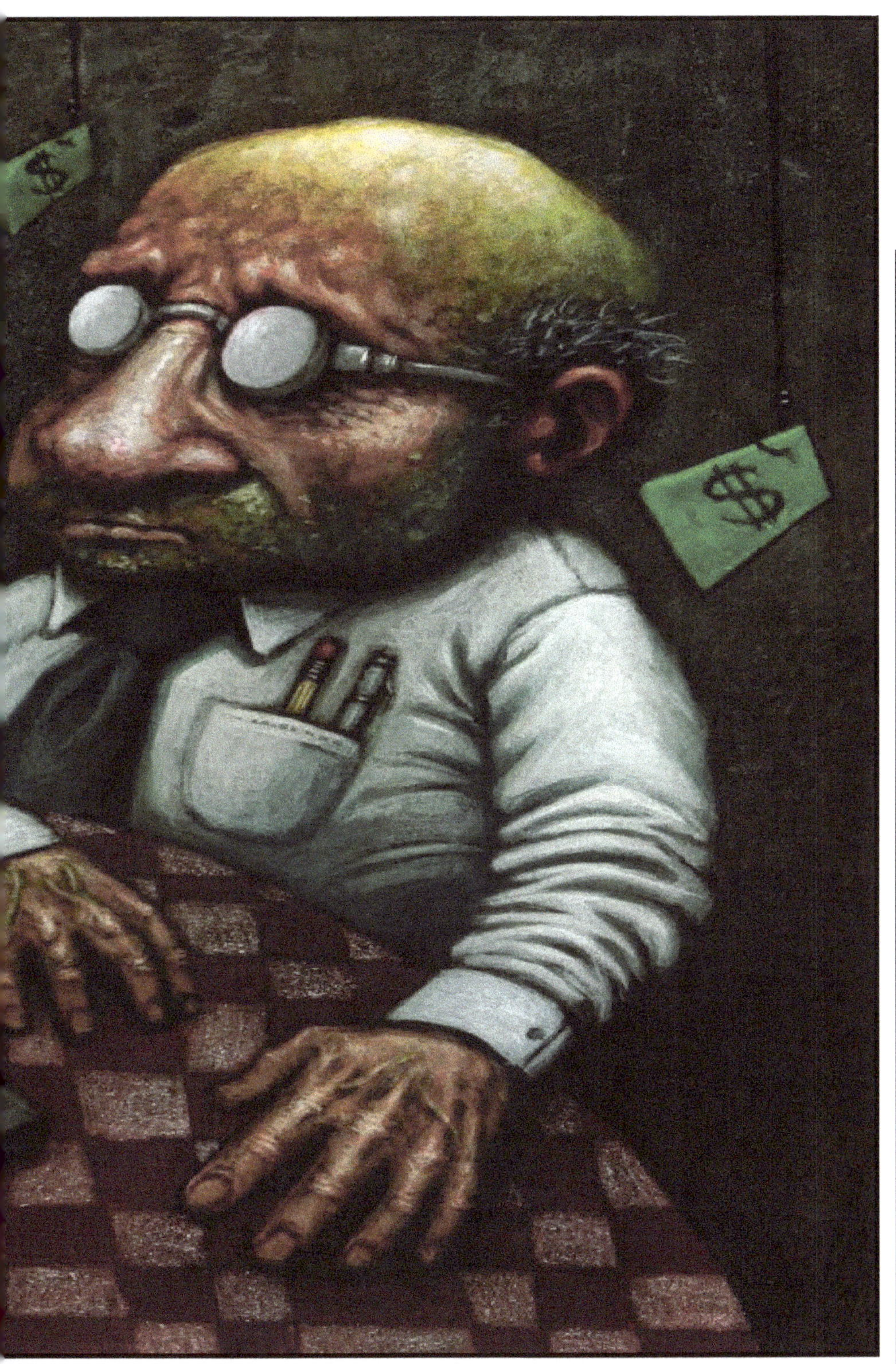

Entropy Portraits

Levi DeMatteo

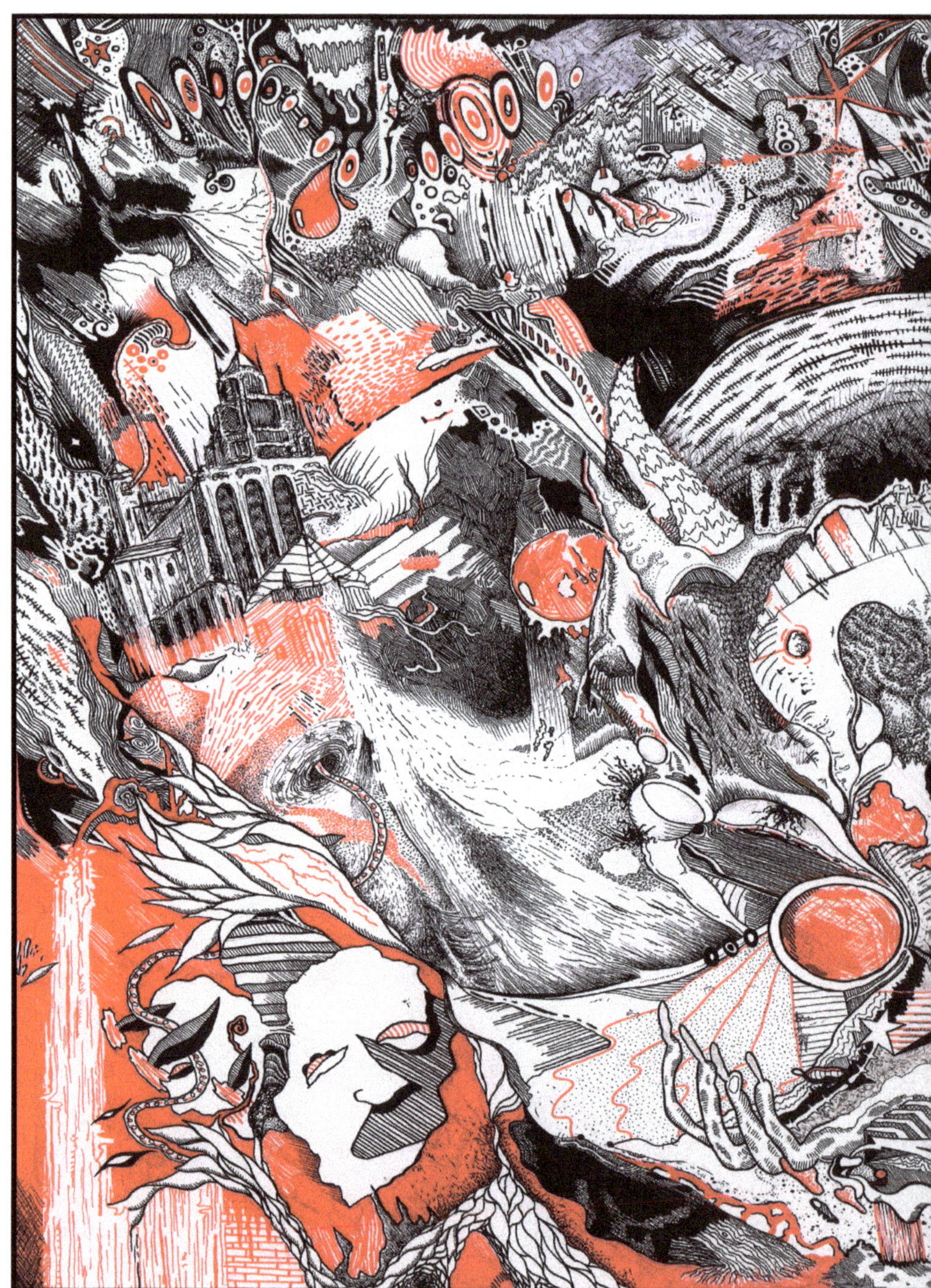

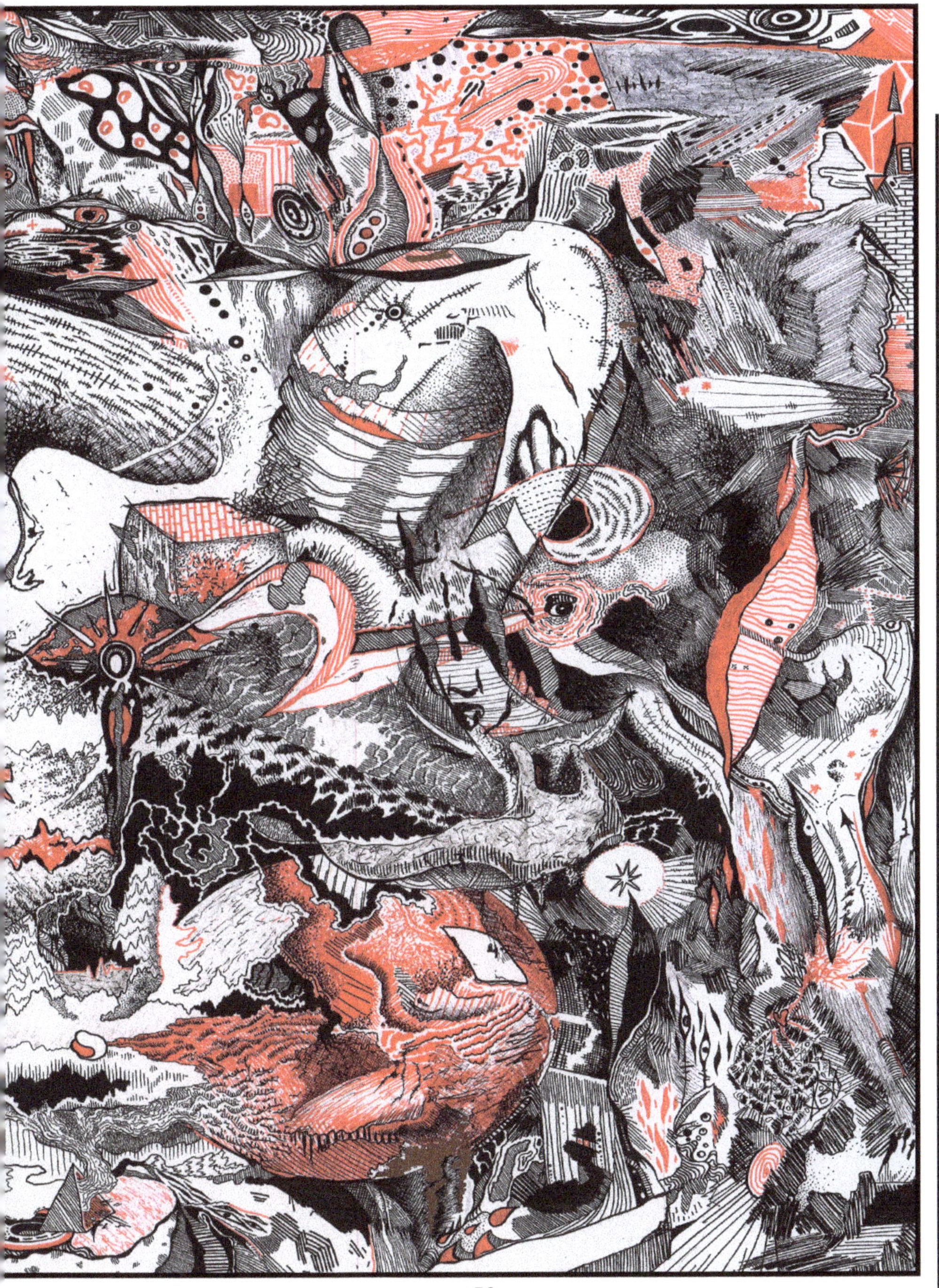

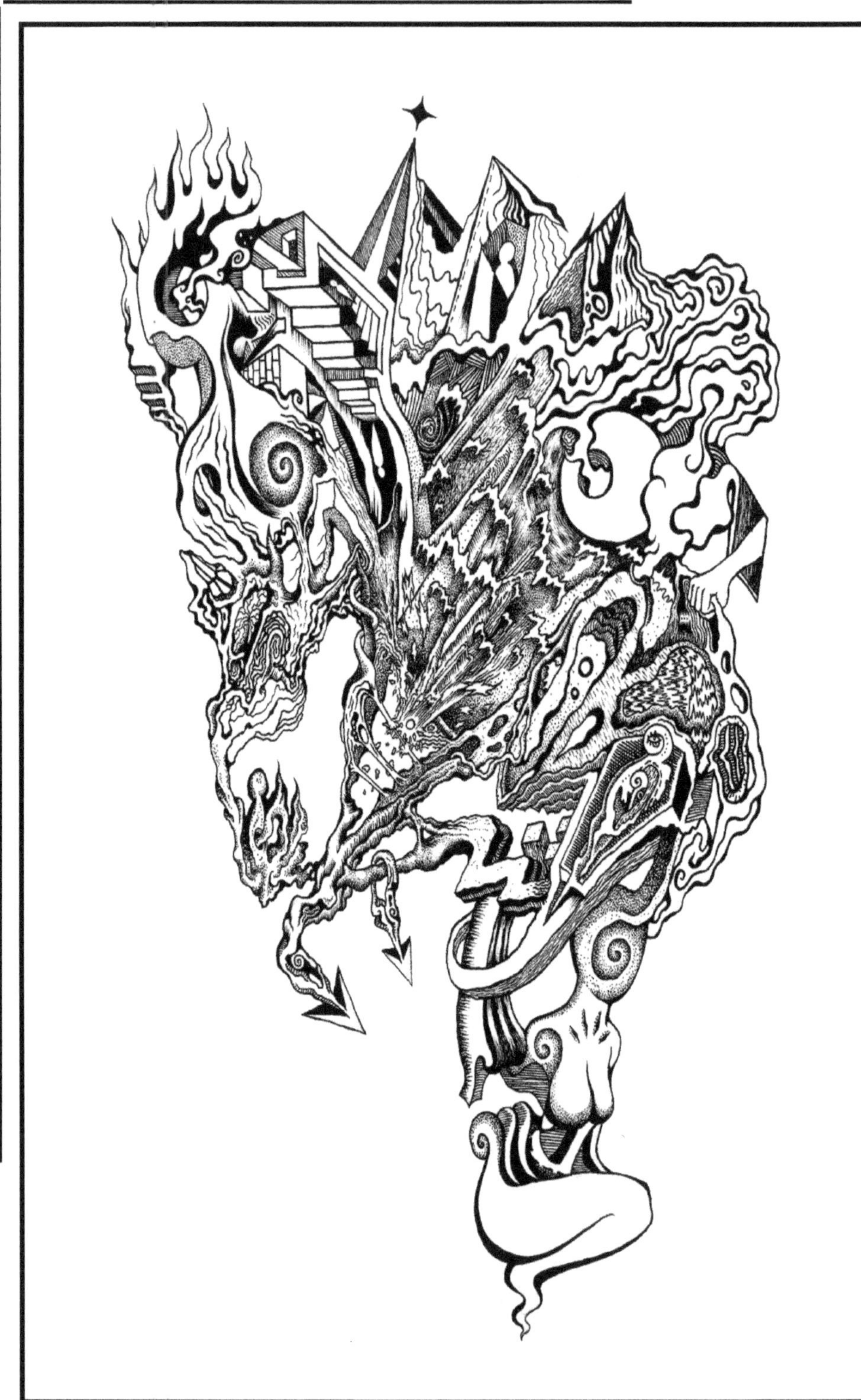

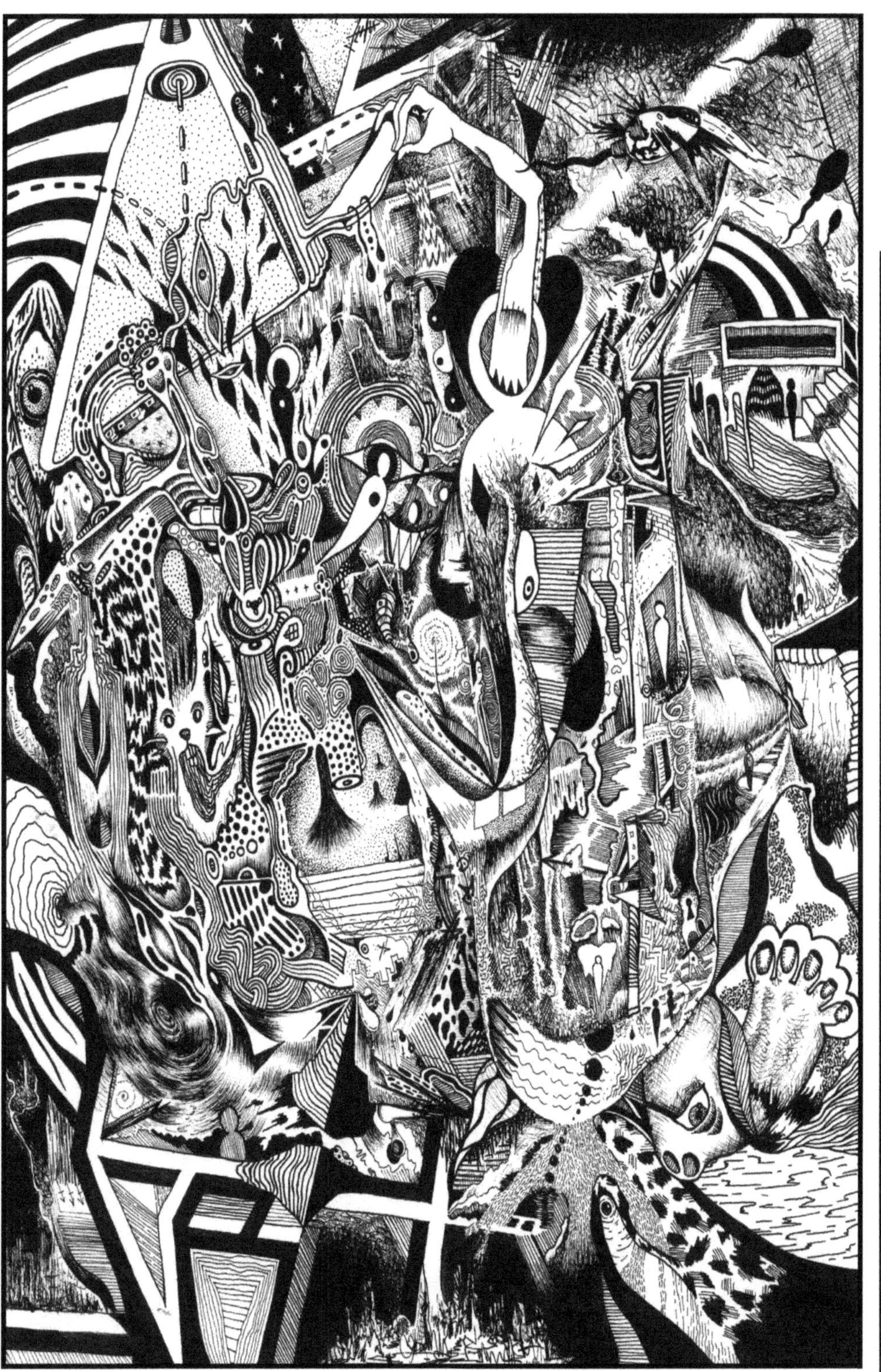

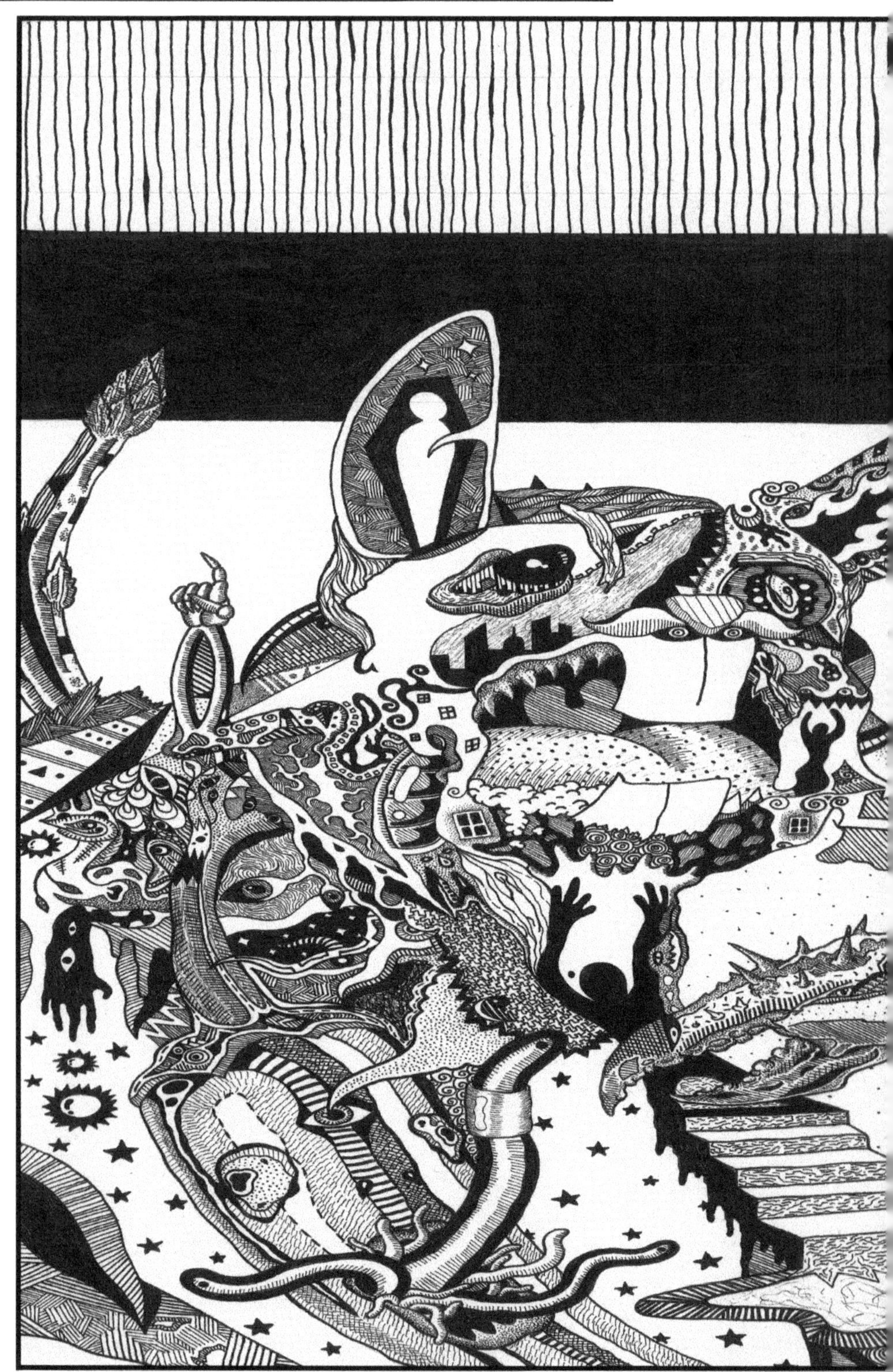

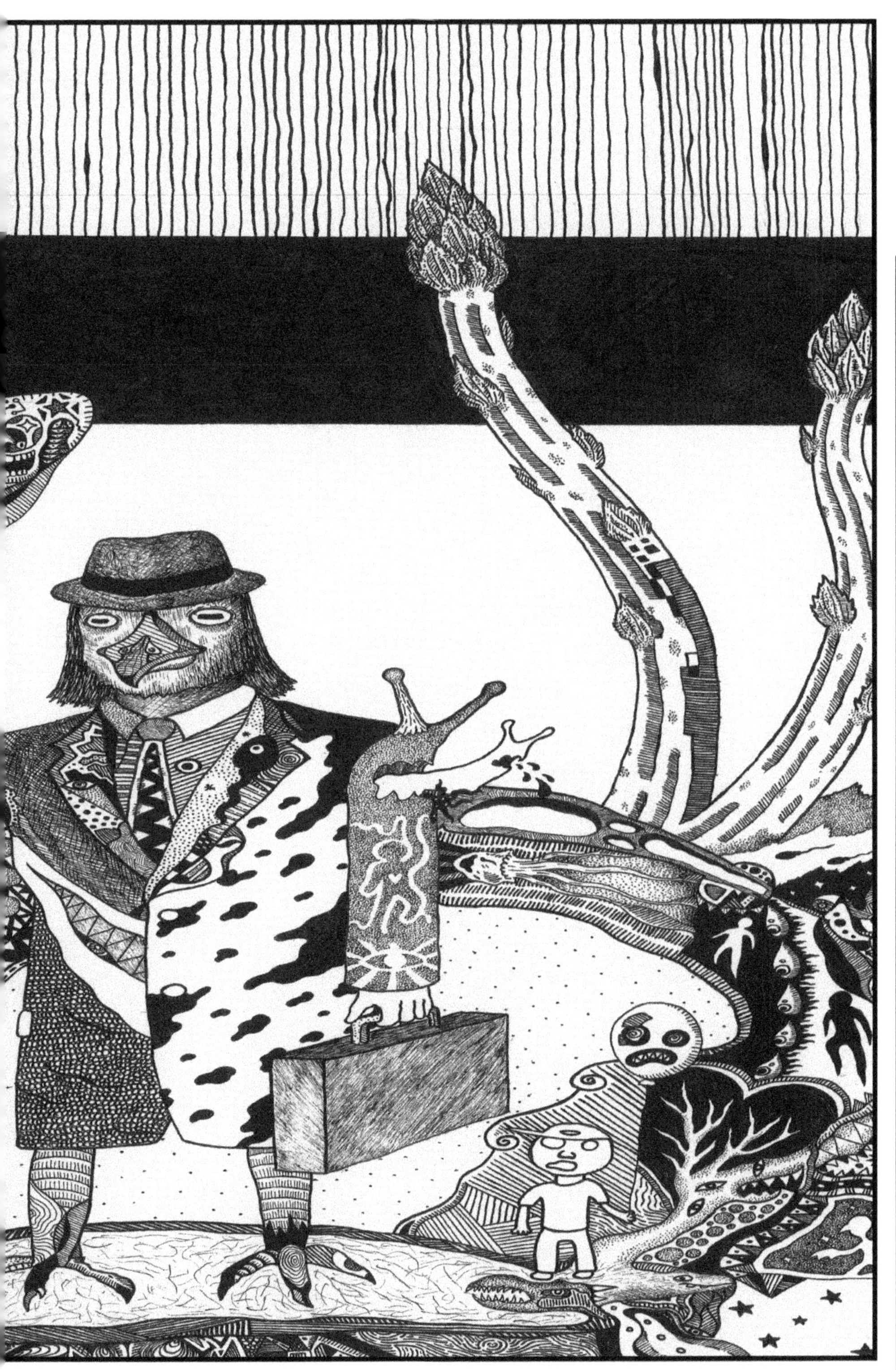

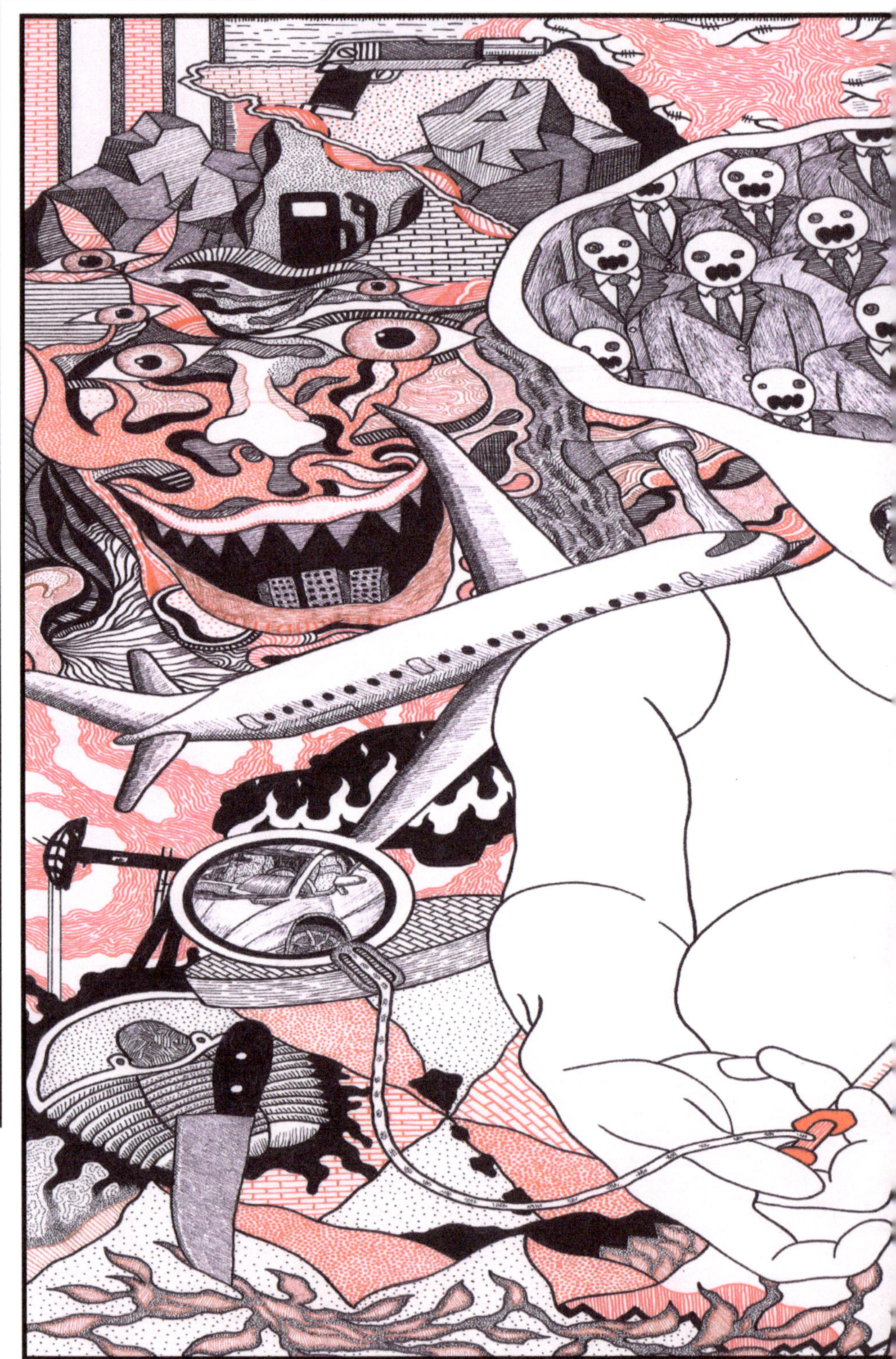

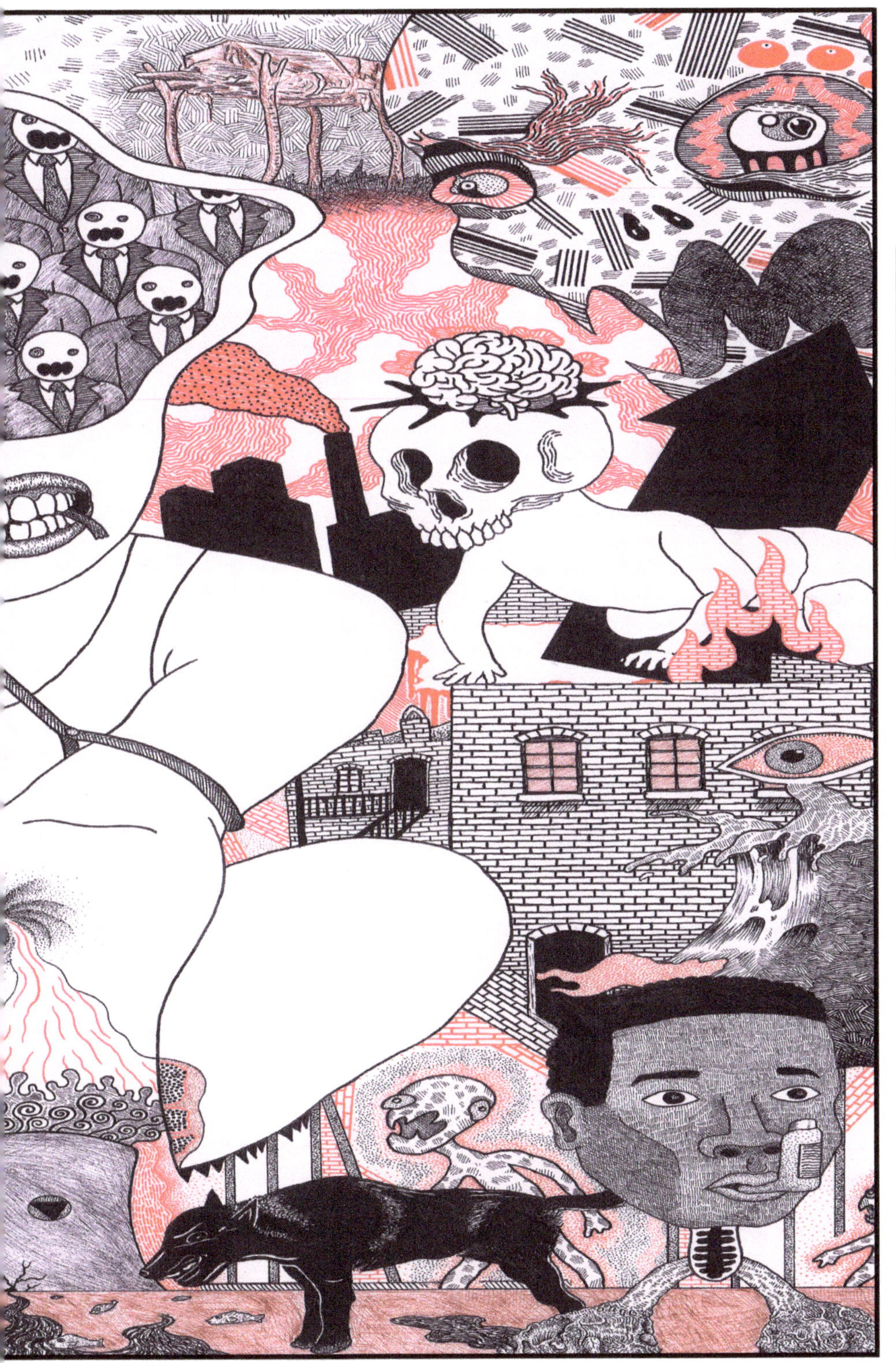

Necropolis

Mugu Ganesan

I scratched the backdoor
until my pale pink claws broke,

I pounded my empty stainless-steel bowl
to bring you back from slumber,

I ran laps around the house hoping
you would sense me,

I licked the rust off the iron railings
on the porch where we had played that evening,

I barked, whimpered,
and howled,

I wrangled hard with the green vine snake,
brawling for one more dawn.

Maybe none of this happened.
how would you know?

The army of ants
leading the funeral out of my ears

narrate: *Yama took me away*
when you failed to hear my voice.

Trolley

Matt Vekakis

First, you feel it in
your bowels—the

creeping familiar
of remembering—

collating out of the
static Maine heat.

Rows of old Pullman-
Standards: green,

orange, blue—
Wonderland still

the indicated
destination. Up

the old staircase
of an Edinburgh

tram—carved out
like an expired

womb. Watch the
dust motes trample

the predicate stillness;
eerie—loneliness

placated only in
howling. Bodies

having filled the
surviving seats

where gashes expose
the compressed

polyester—spilling
out like intestines;

father doesn't
speak of Vietnam,

and I don't speak
of what I've done

to get here.

TRANSUBSTANTIATION

Jessica Manack

You filled me in the way you were allowed:
a bowl of steaming curry, double-forked.
We'd cancel all our meetings for the day
and I'd ride in your car, gaily bedorked,

a blur, so fast no one could trace our steps,
to the strip mall with the Thai place no one liked.
And neither of us touched a single phone.
And neither of us thought about your wife.

We laughed and laughed, our best stories unfurled,
and snuck back to our desks two hours late.
My eyes would gleam, embarrassed with delight.
My cheeks were pinked with Spicy Level 8,

My crevices prepped, smooth and jasmine-ripe,
in case this was the day things took a turn.
You never touched me and I don't know why.
Was there a lesson I had failed to learn?

Were you as scared as I to take a step?
Or keeping me a dangling backup plan?
Why had I confused you for a god,
You spiceless, frightened noodle of a man?

Falling into a Pot

Emory Schuett

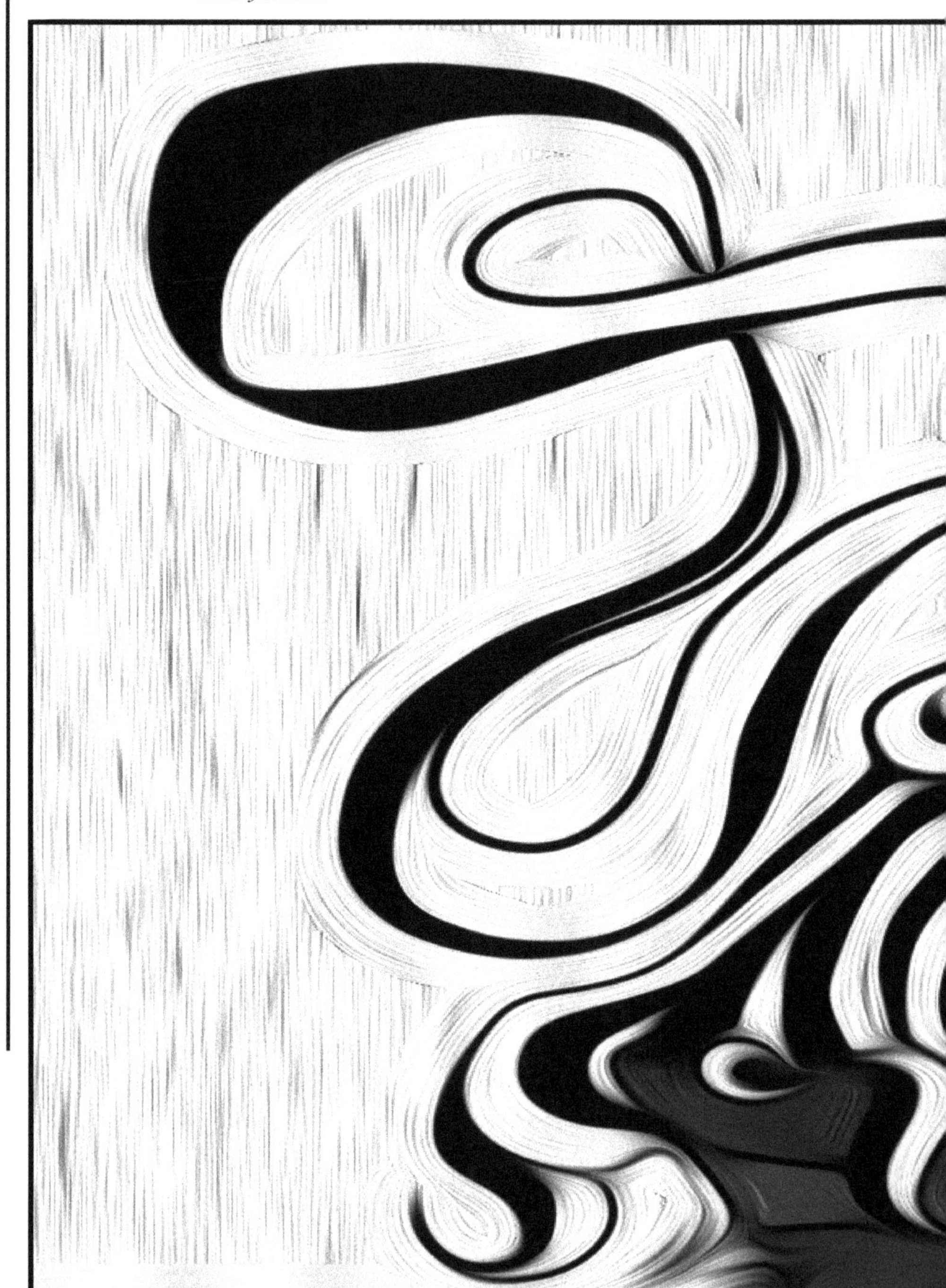

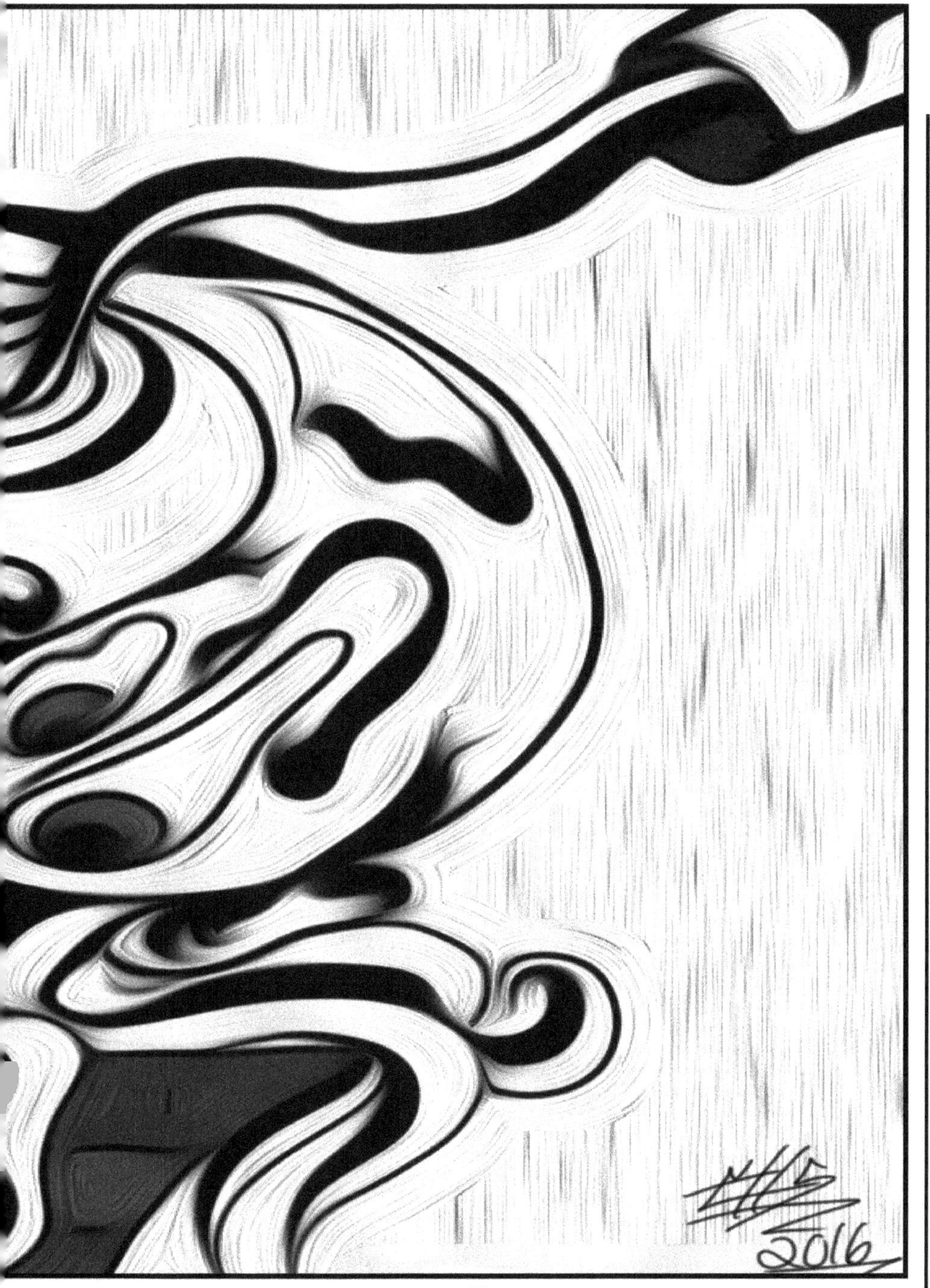
2016

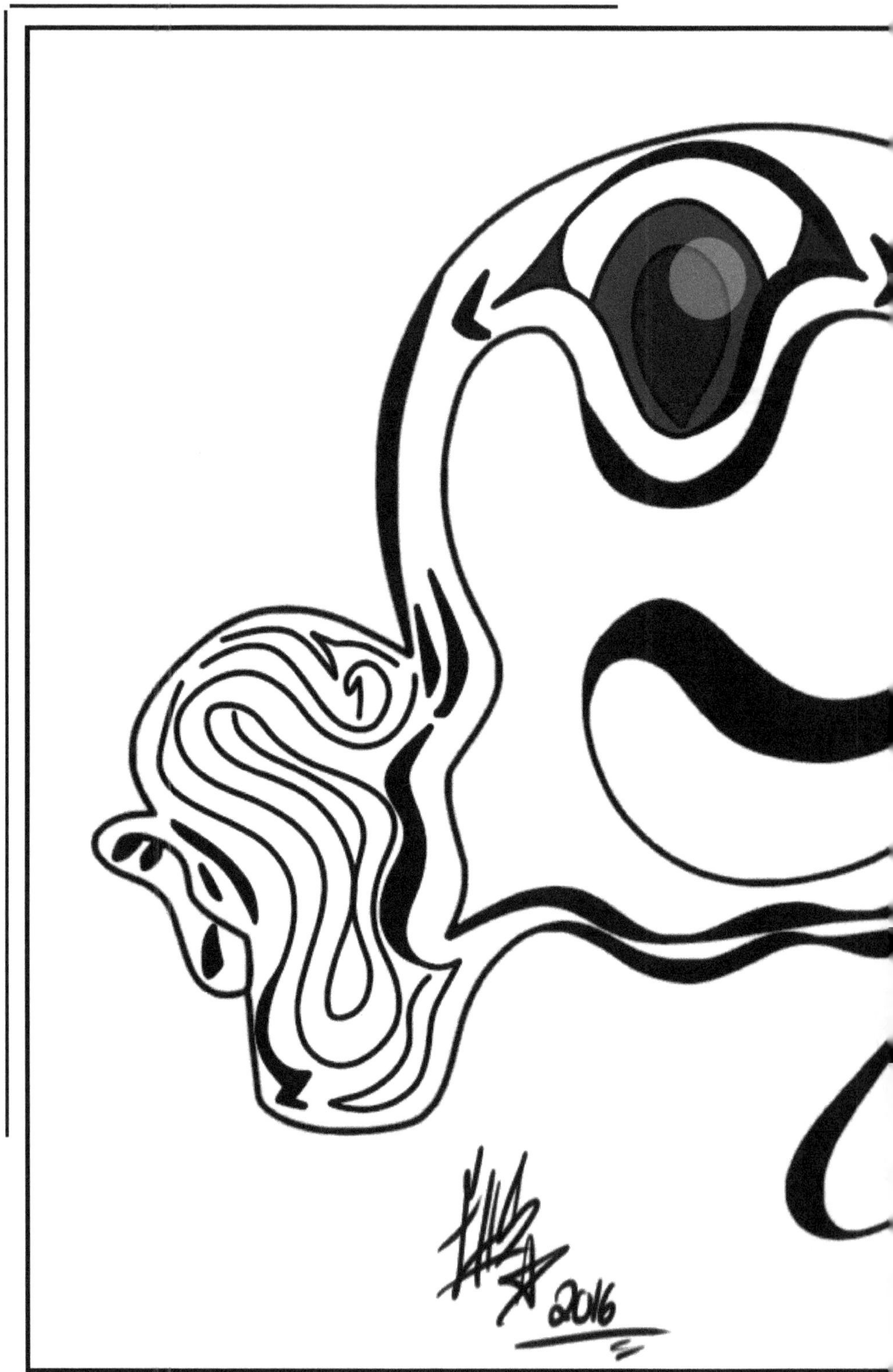

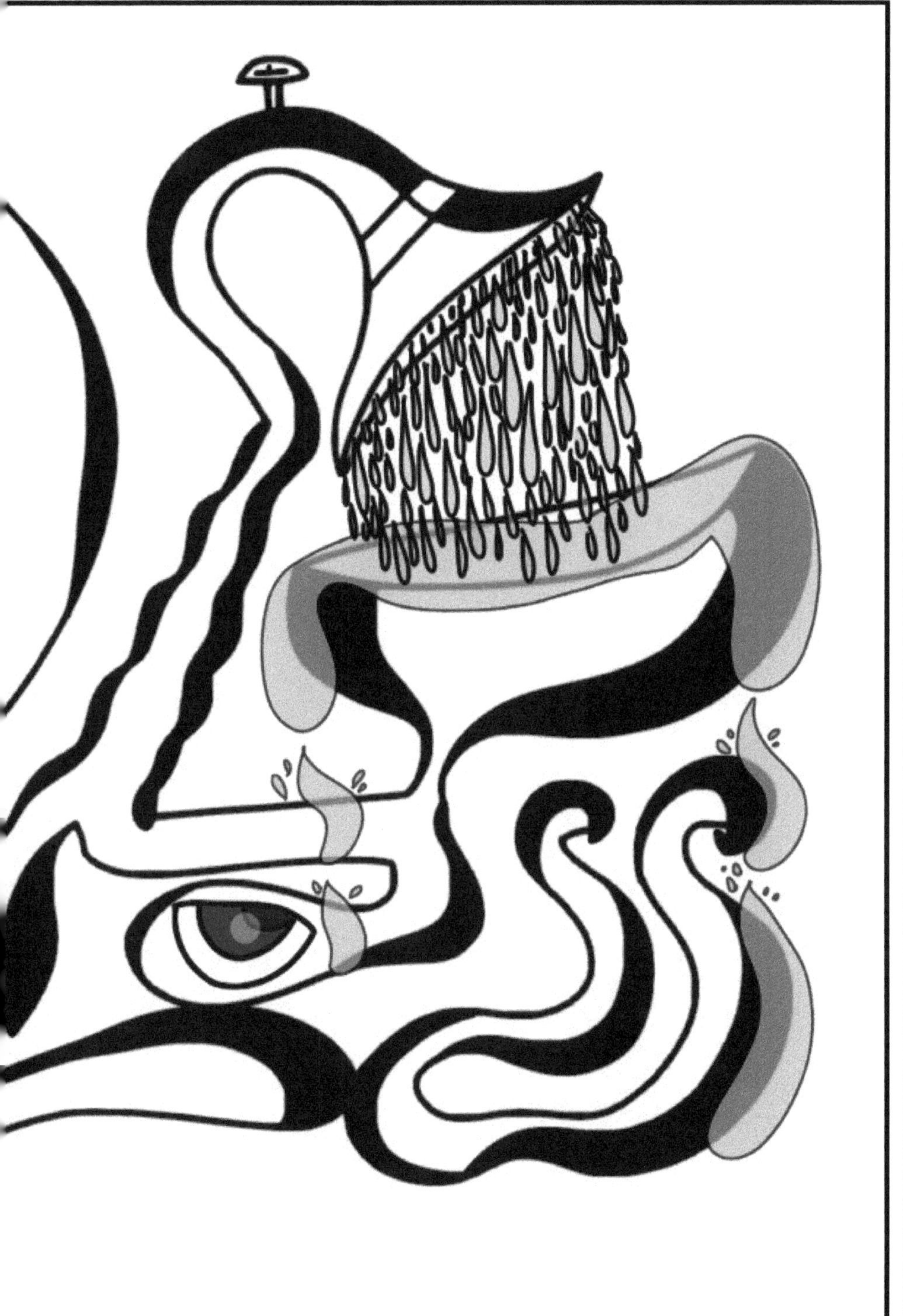

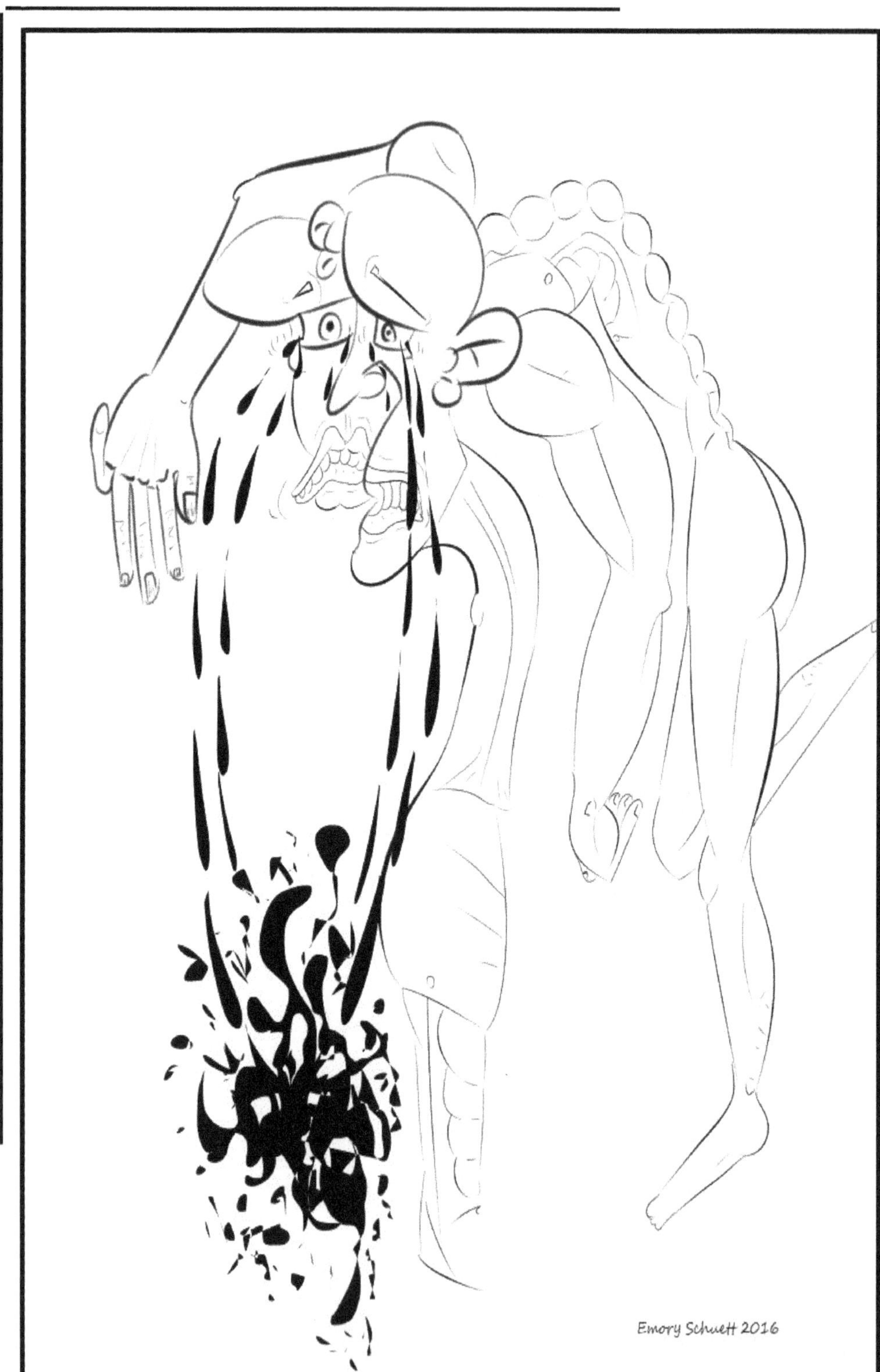
Emory Schuett 2016

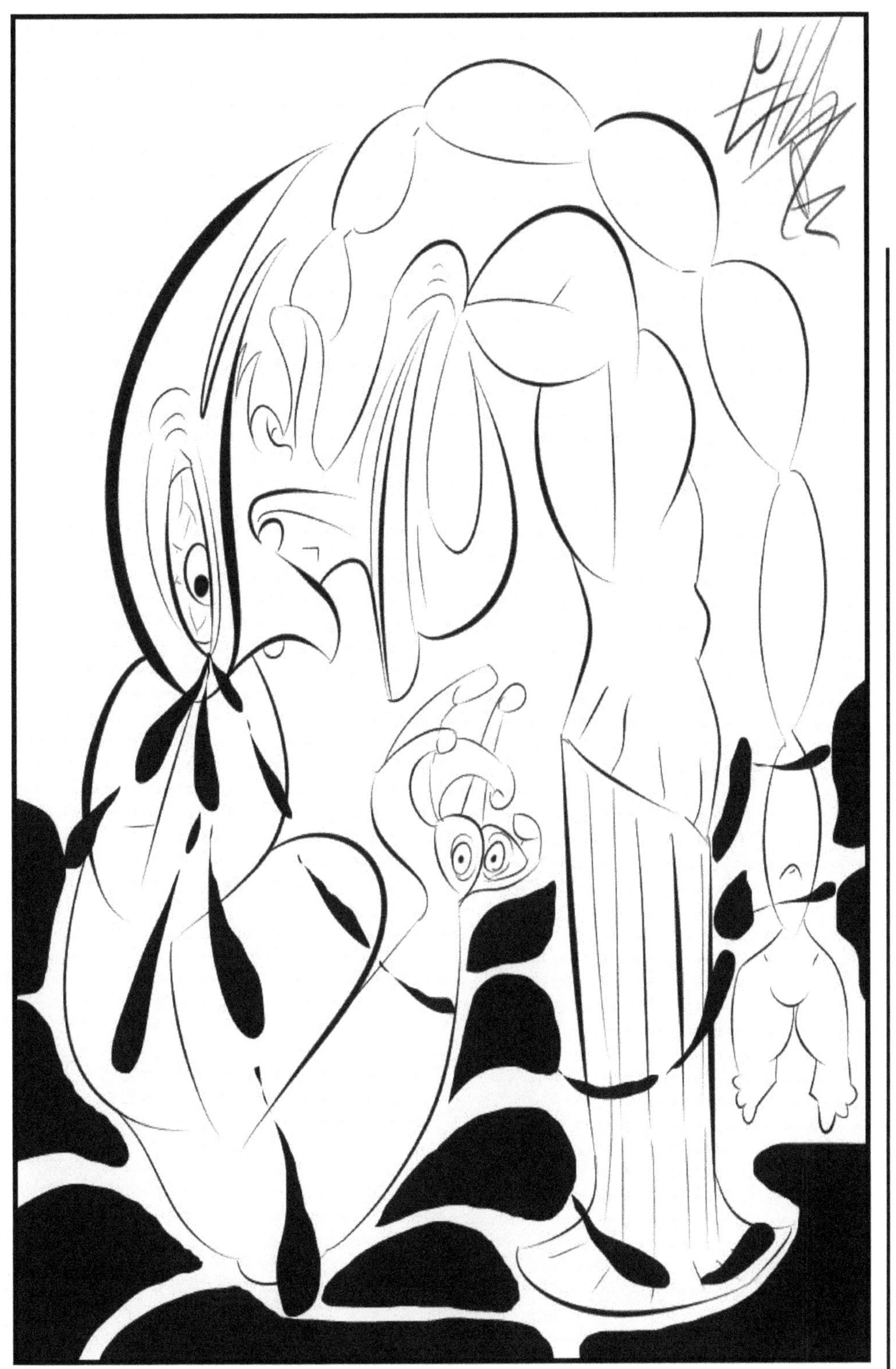

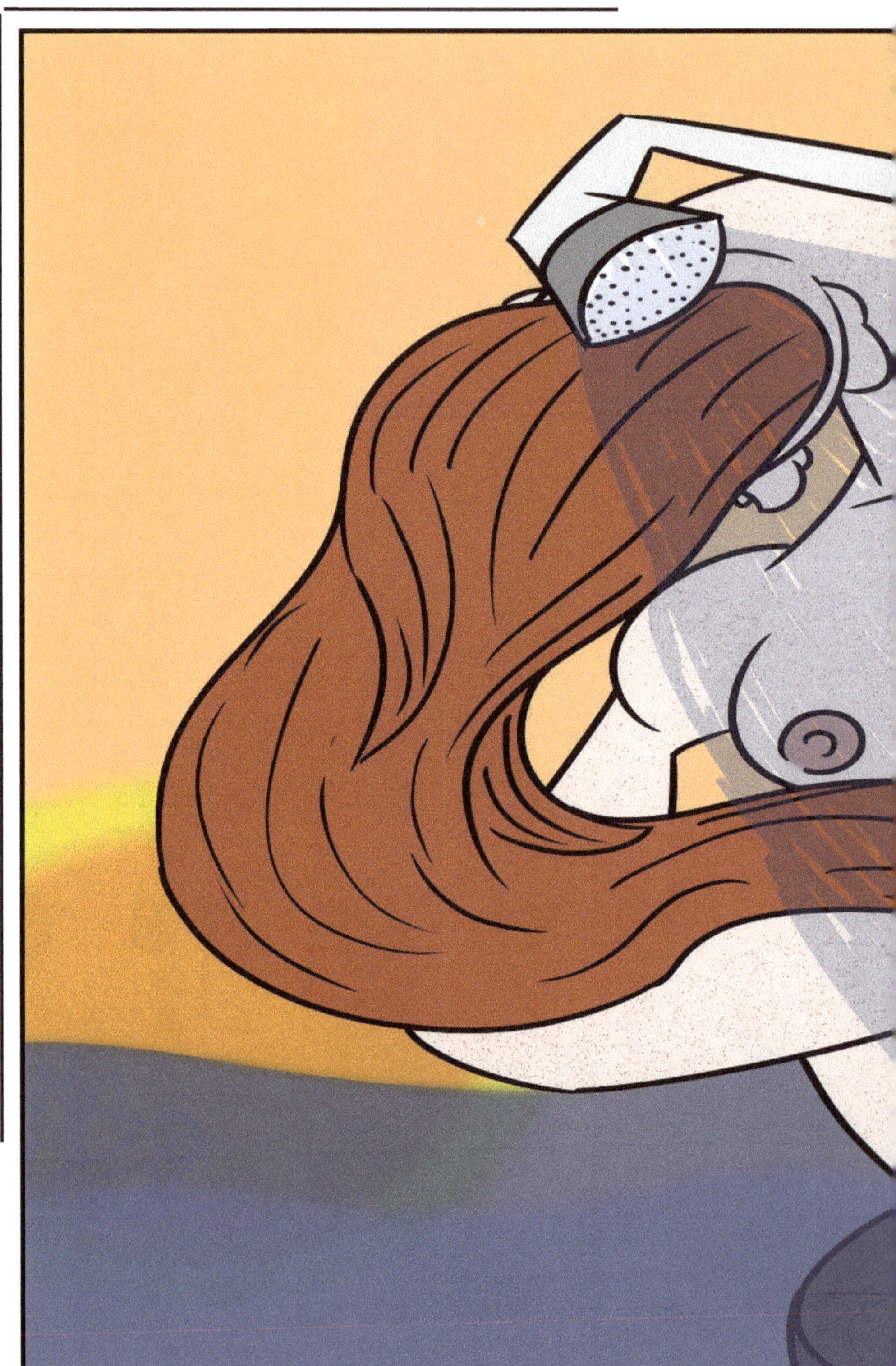

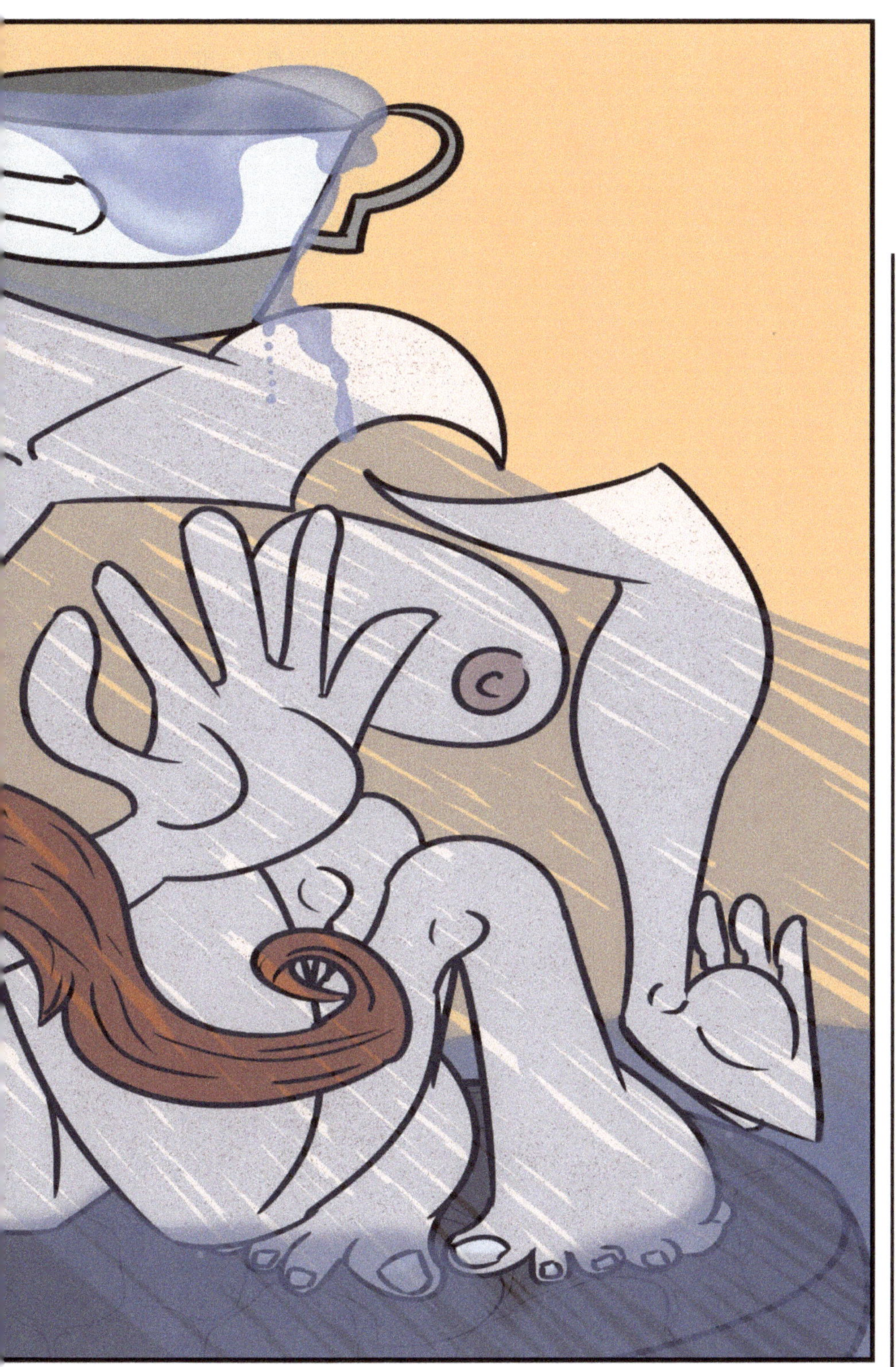

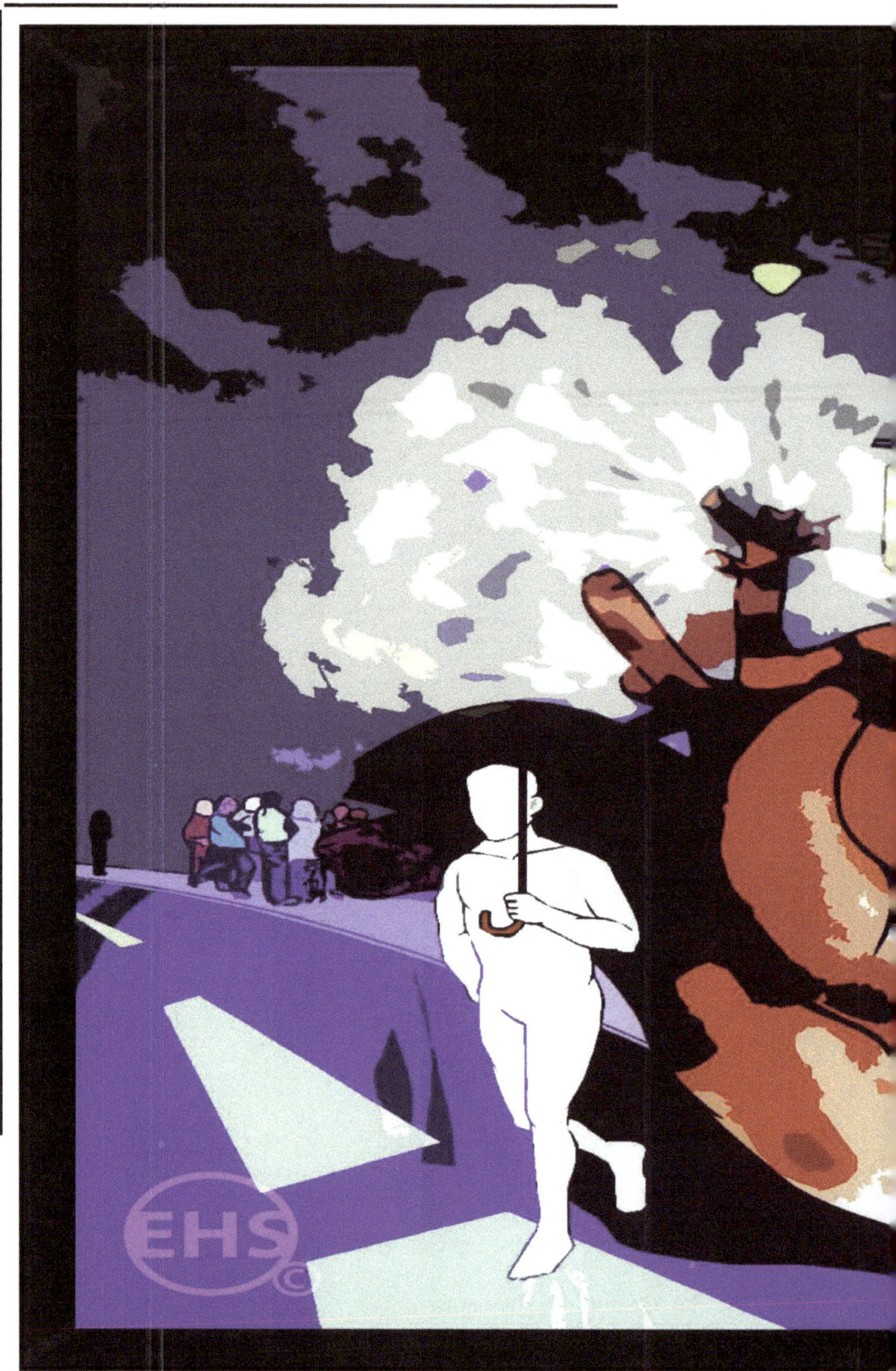

EHS

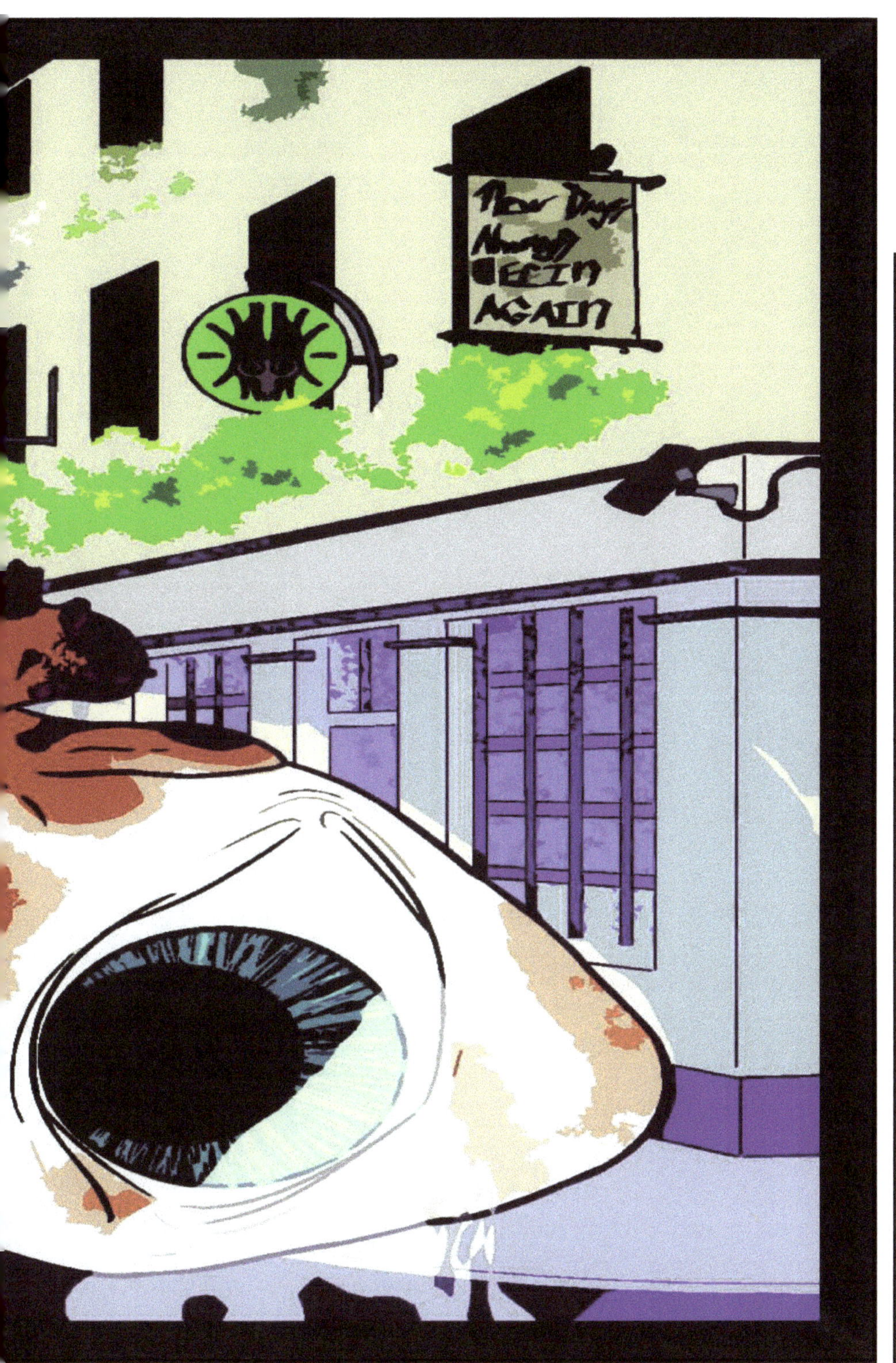
New Days
Never
BEEIN
AGAIN

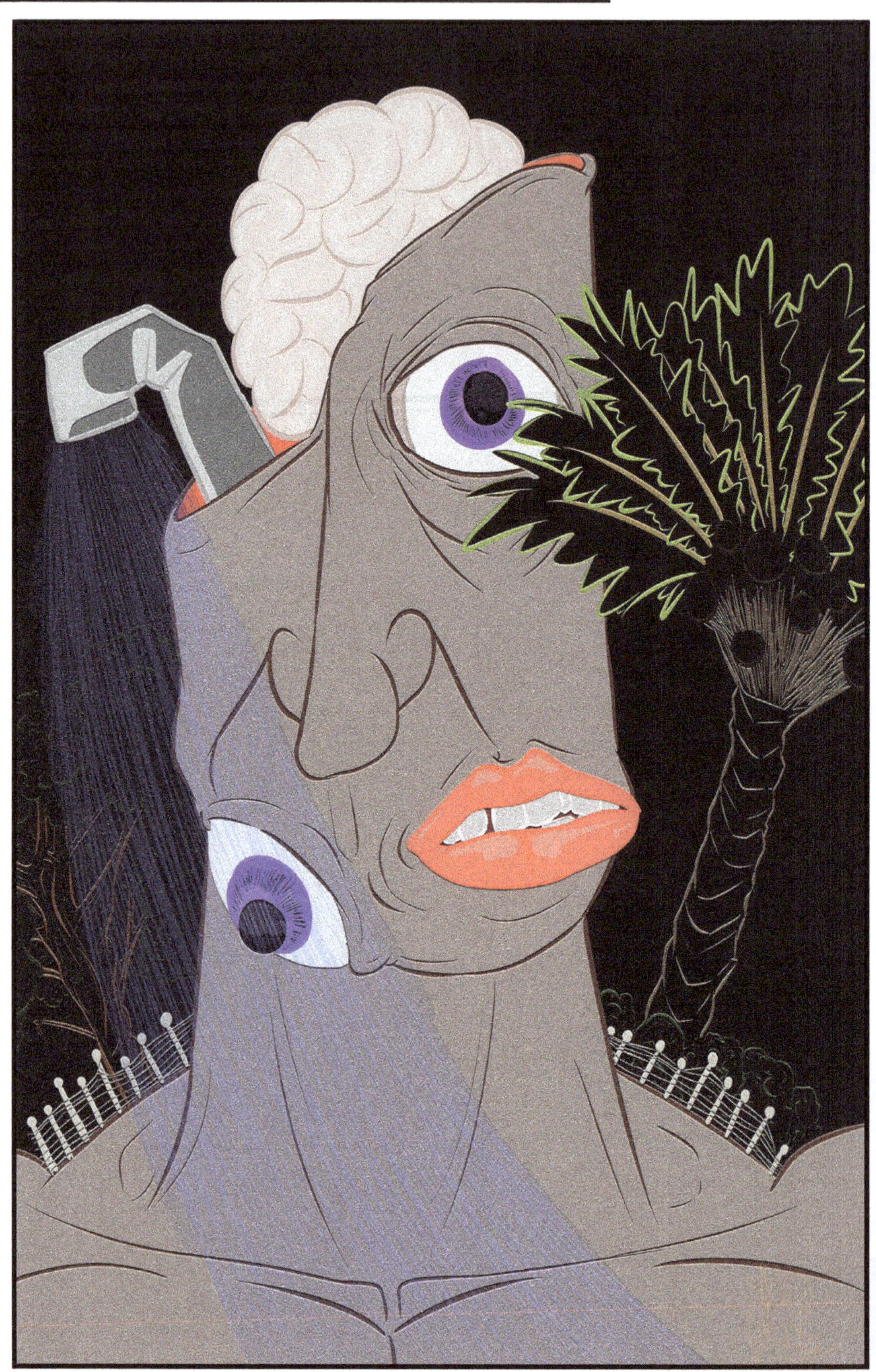

On Love

Andi Talbot

I thought she liked me
when she cooked breakfast
the first morning I was there

pancakes with bacon and maple syrup

by day three
I was awake and up before her,
making the coffee,
washing dishes,
taking out the rubbish
feeding her two dogs.

but always,
she would make breakfast.

I thought she loved me,
when she offered to run me a bath,
and I was greeted with Epsom salts,
a bottle of beer,
and an inexplicable quantity
of freshly lit candles

But it wasn't until the end of the first month,
that I knew.
I knew for sure that she loved me.

Still with the coffee
Still with the pancakes
and the bacon
and the maple syrup
and the hot baths
with beer
and salts
and freshly lit candles

One night,
I had just got out of the bath,
she came and
creeped up behind me
pinched at the skin at the top of my back
and said
"I've been wanting to pop that for days".

Sun Doll...

Dustin Hyman

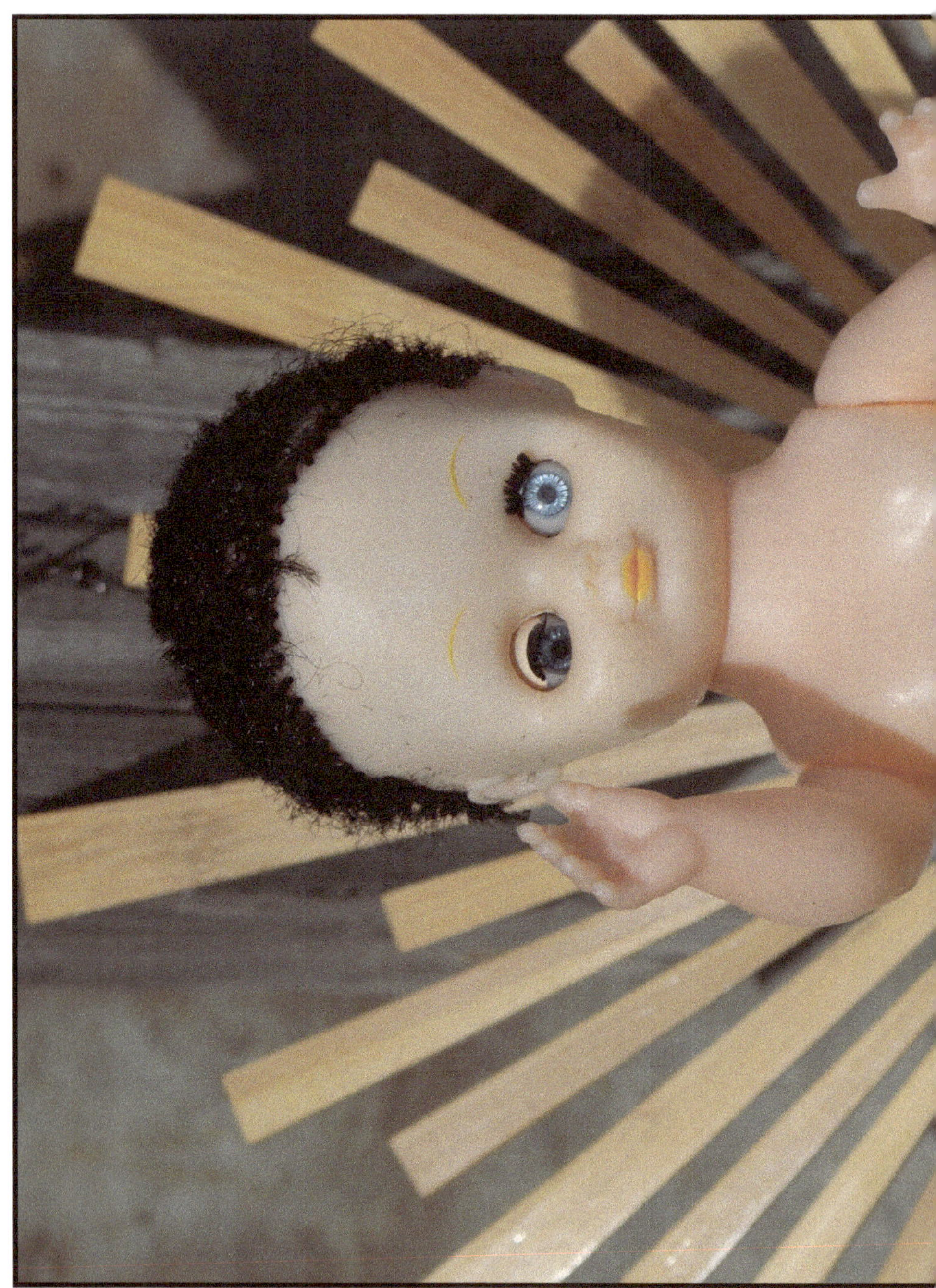

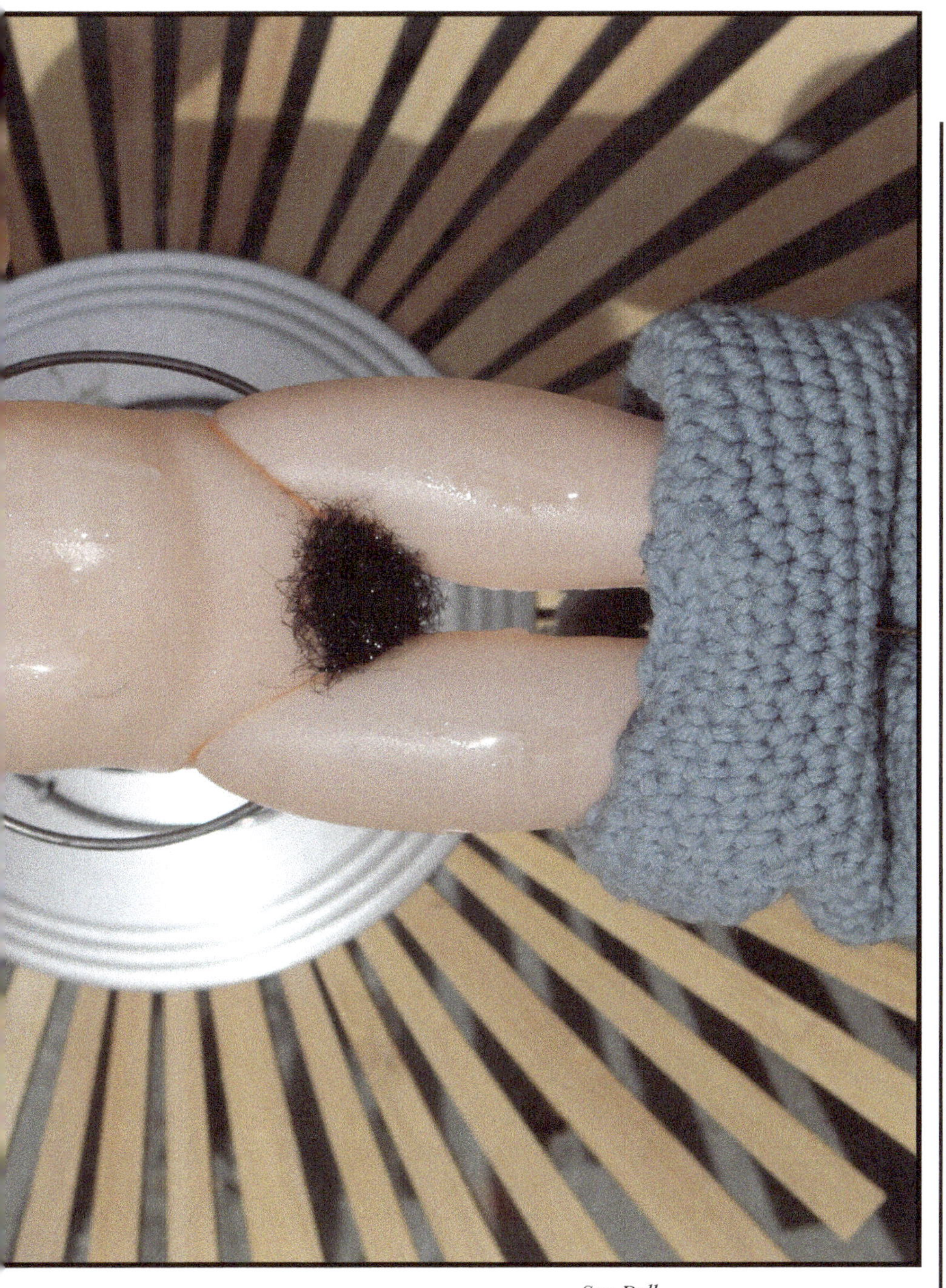

Sun Doll

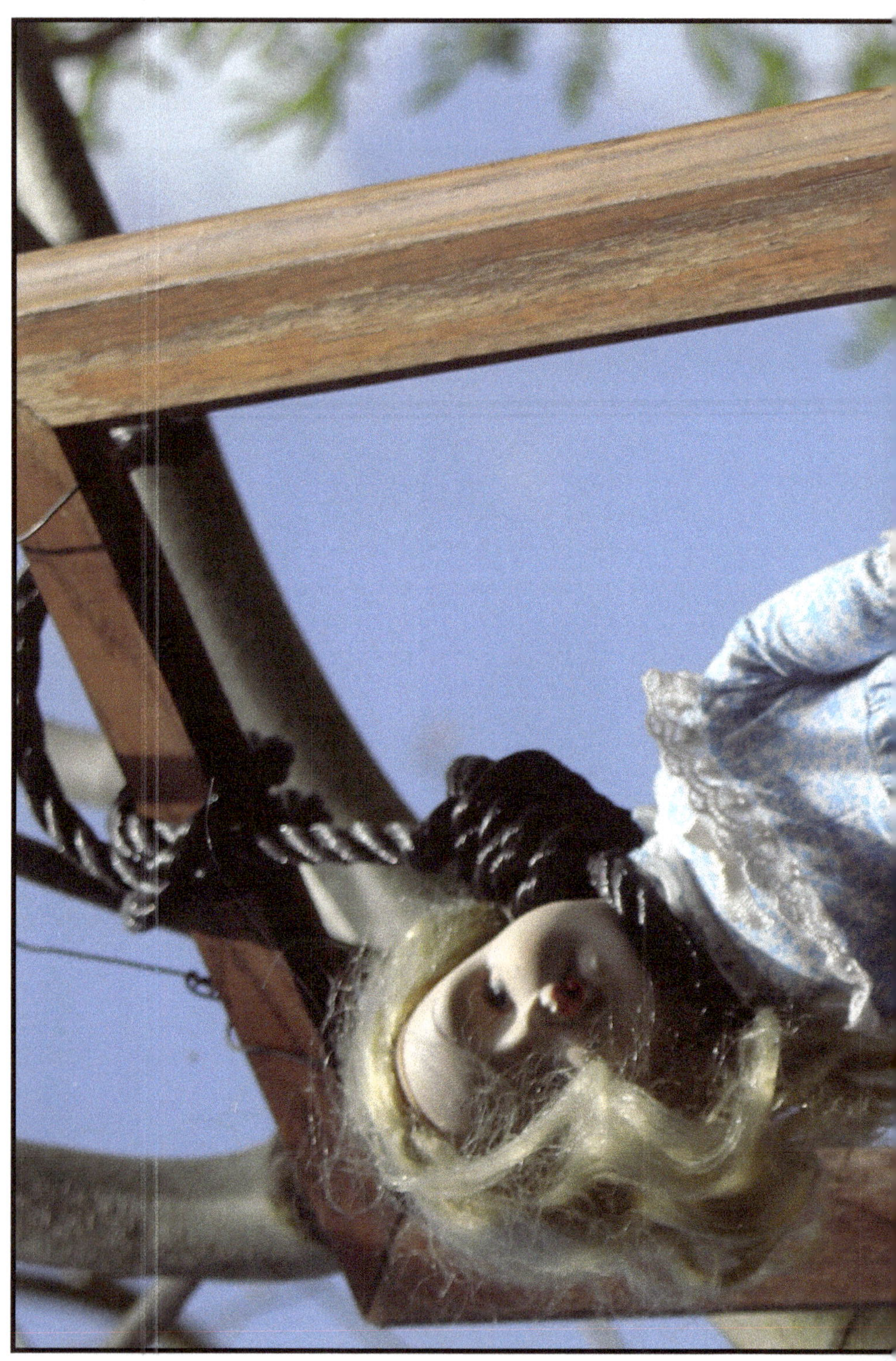

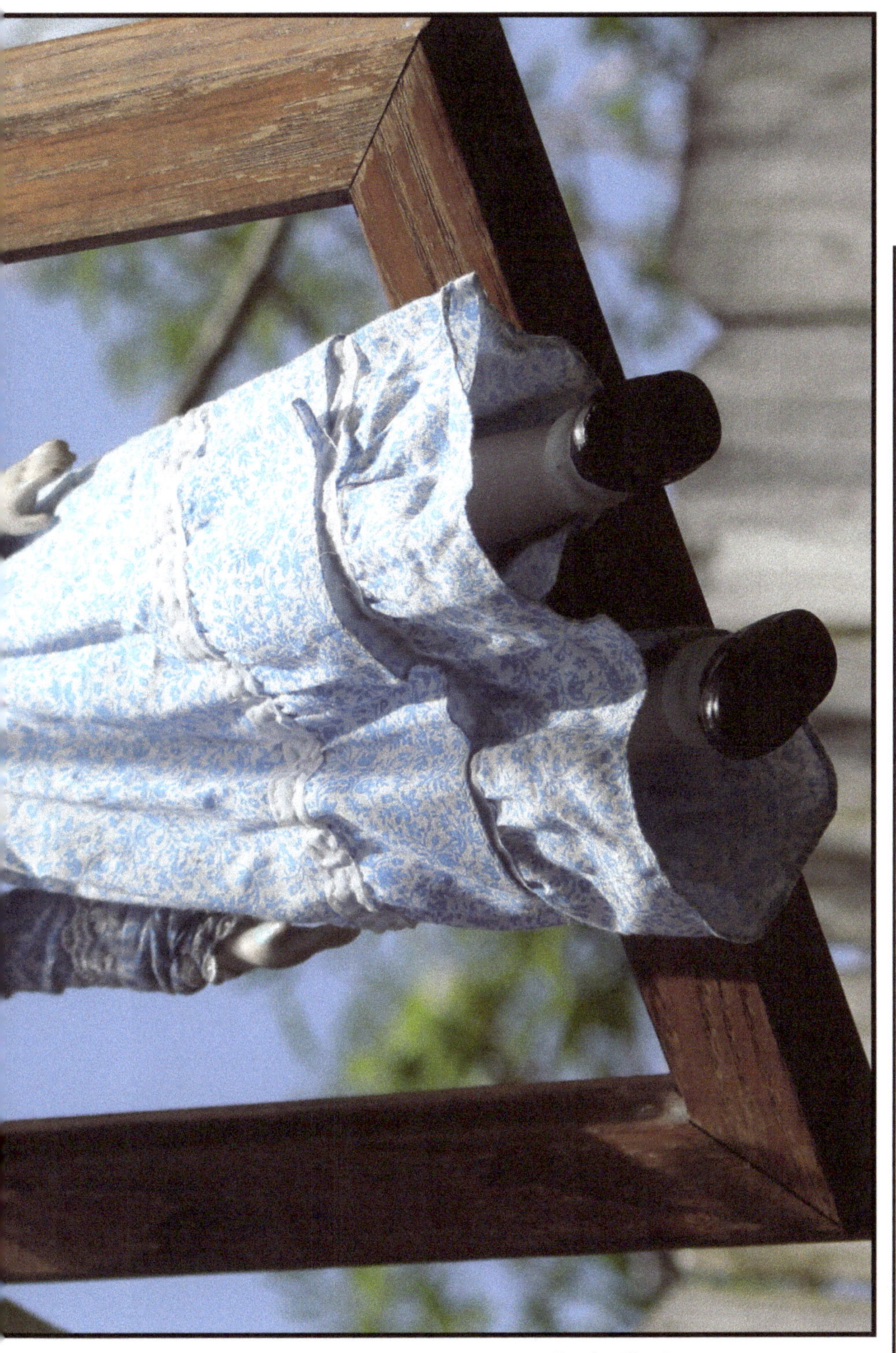

Powder Blue Day

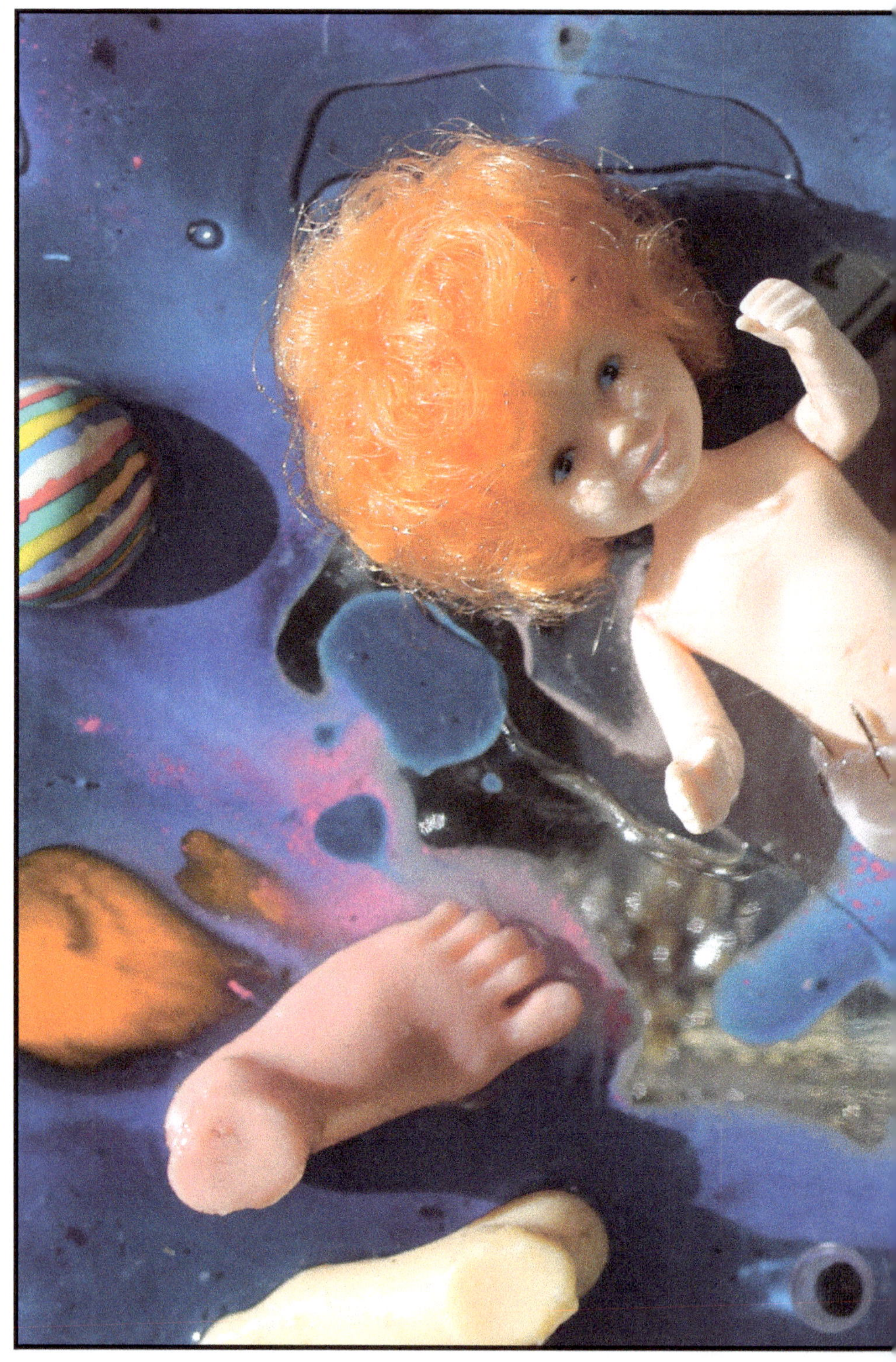

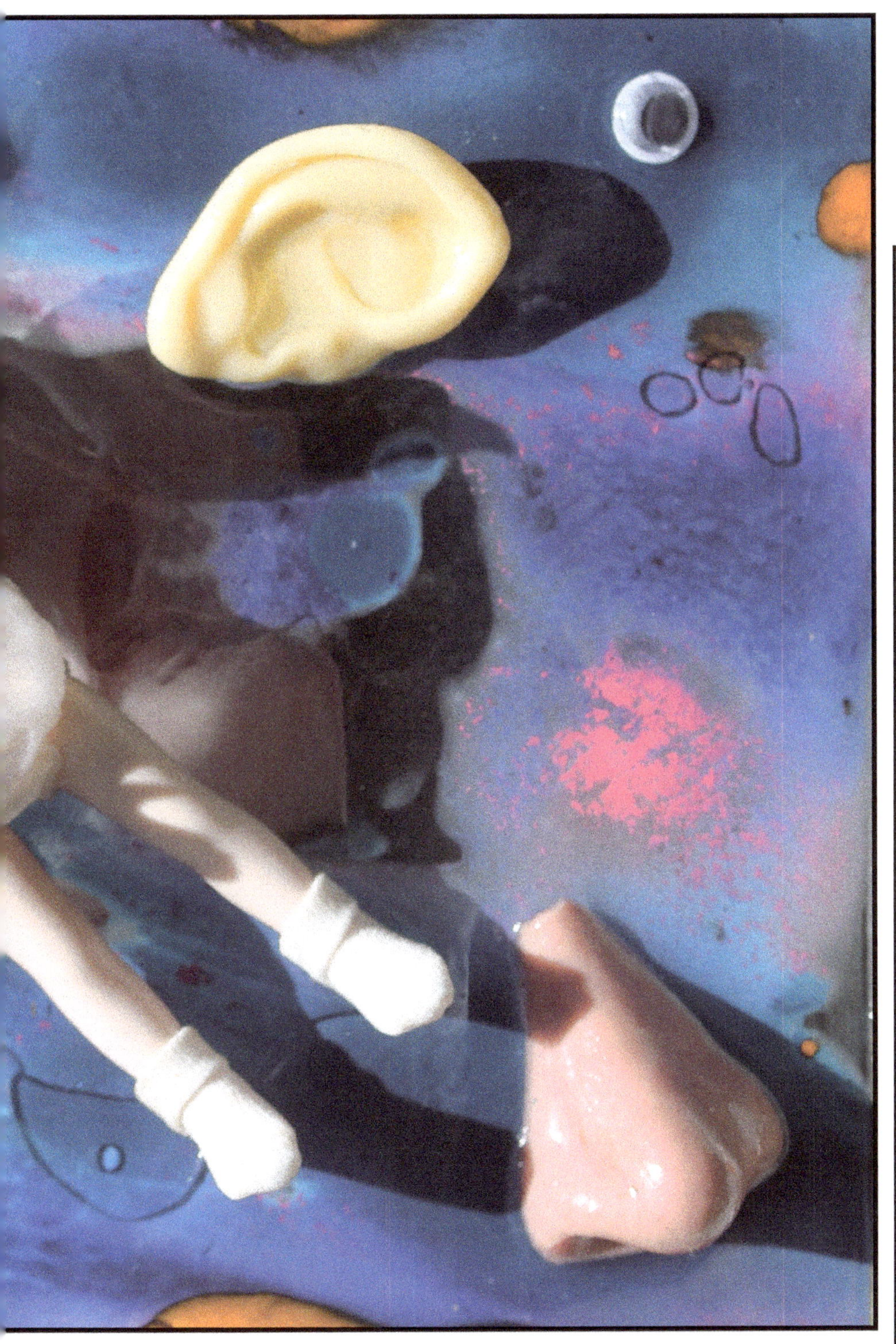

Annie in Glass

Out Of This World

Tony Murray

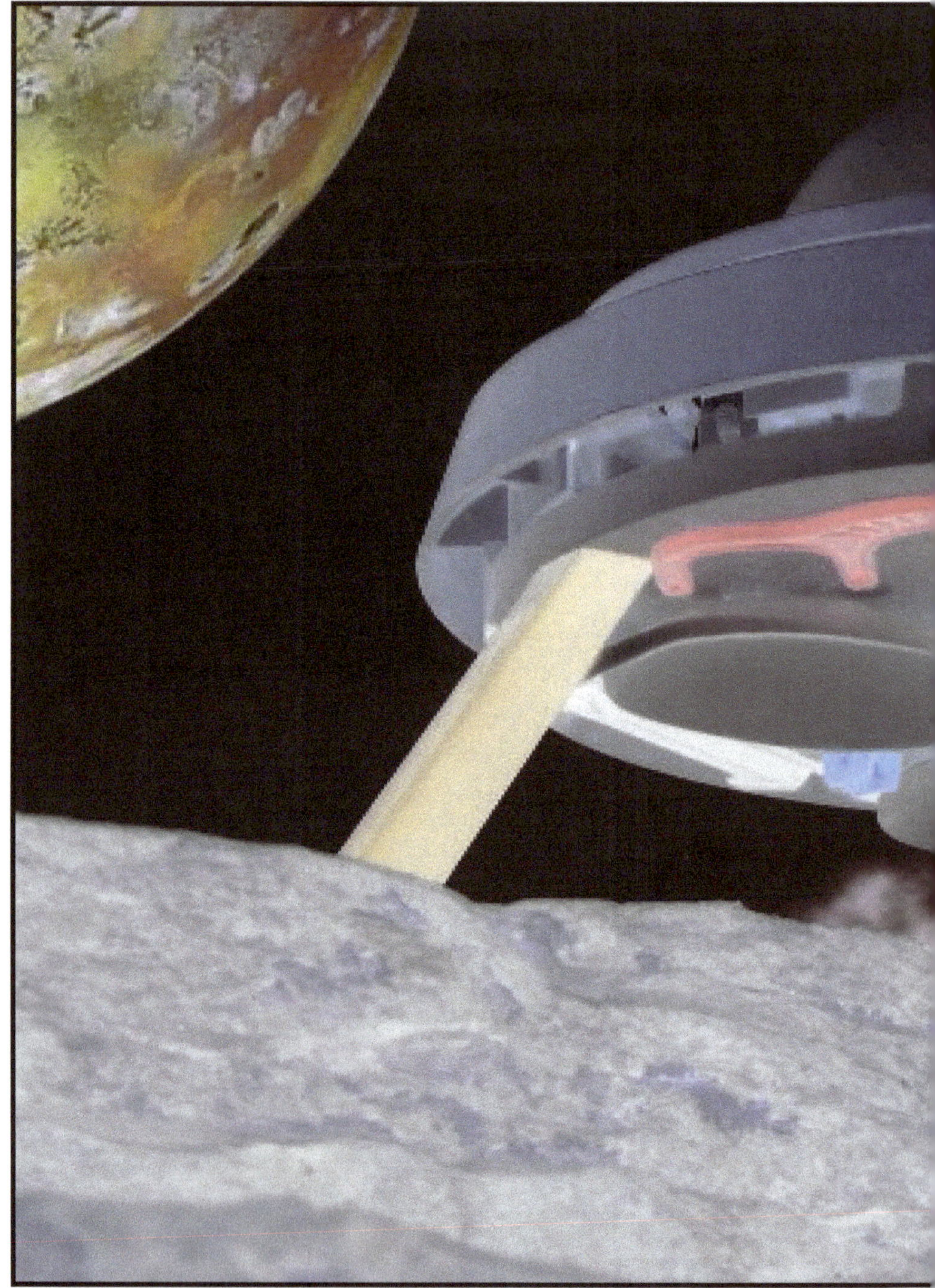

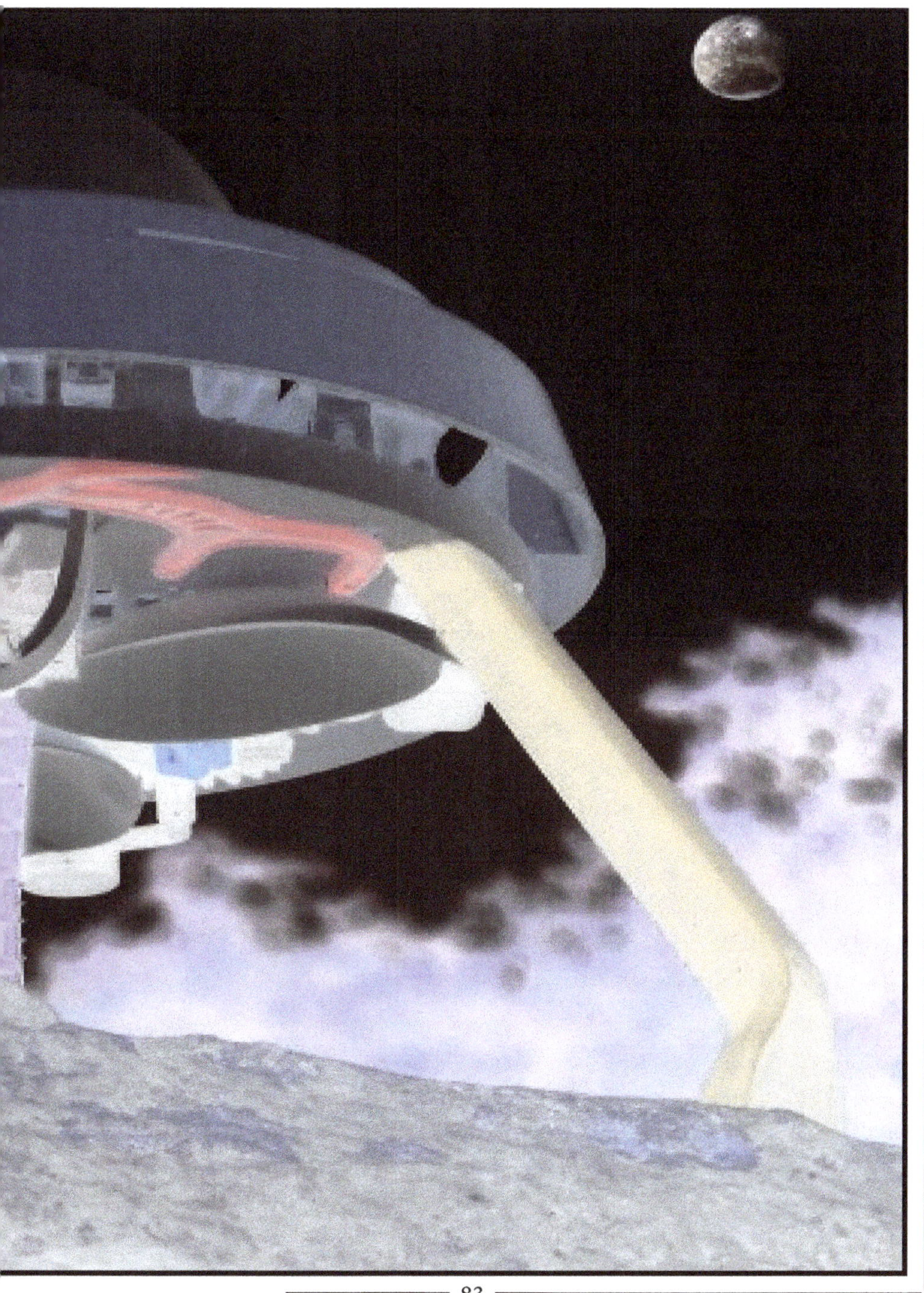

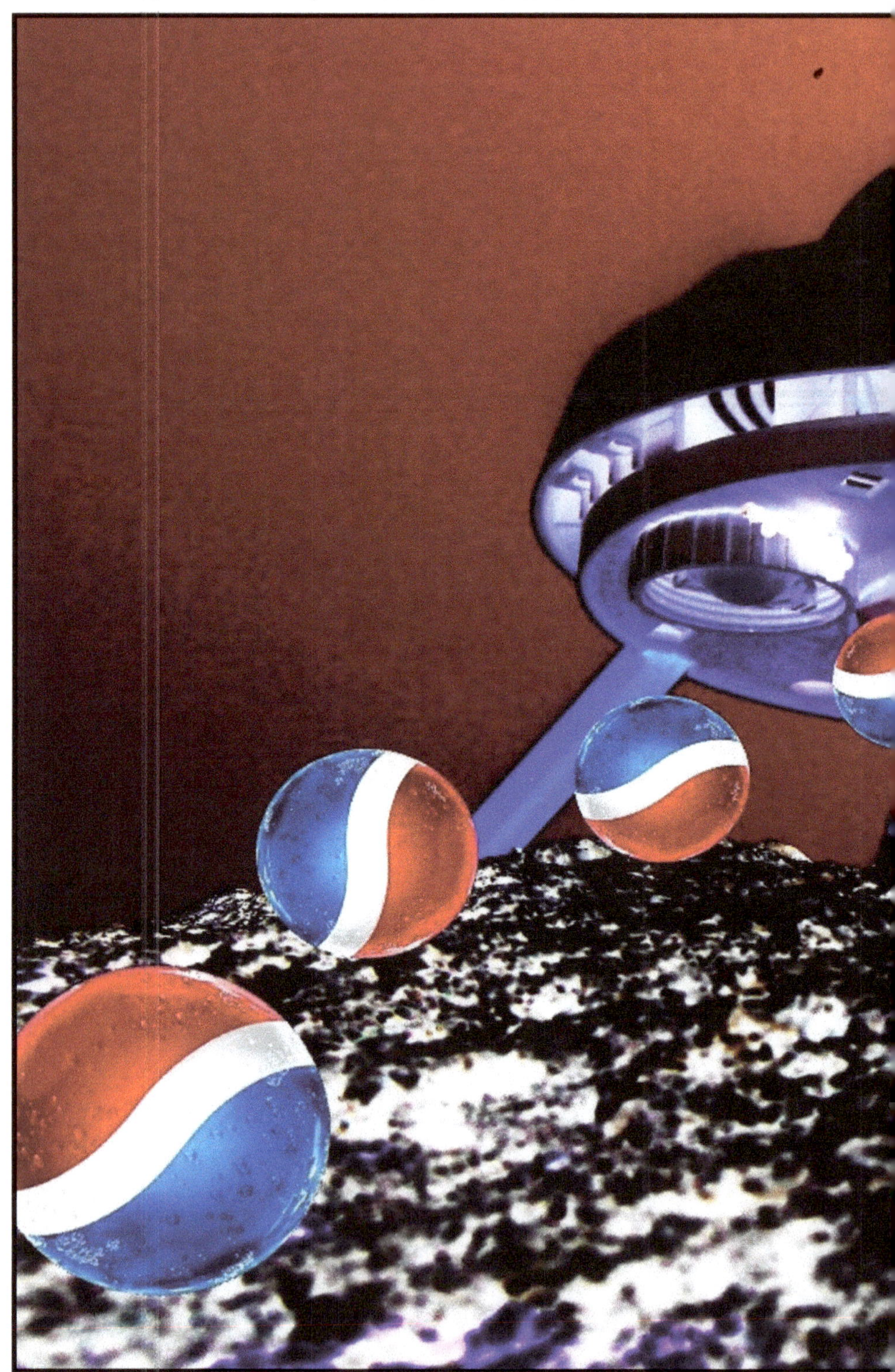

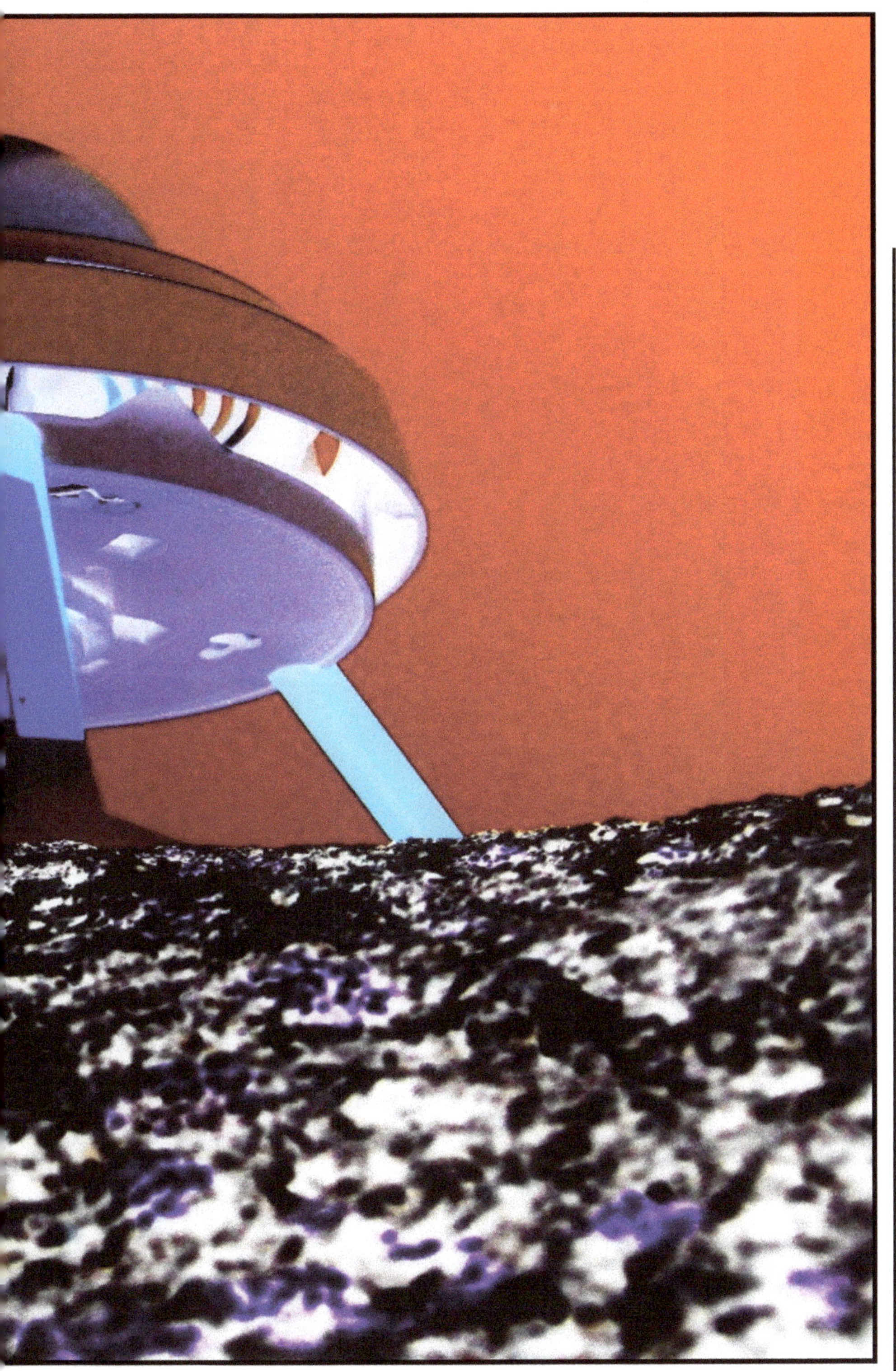

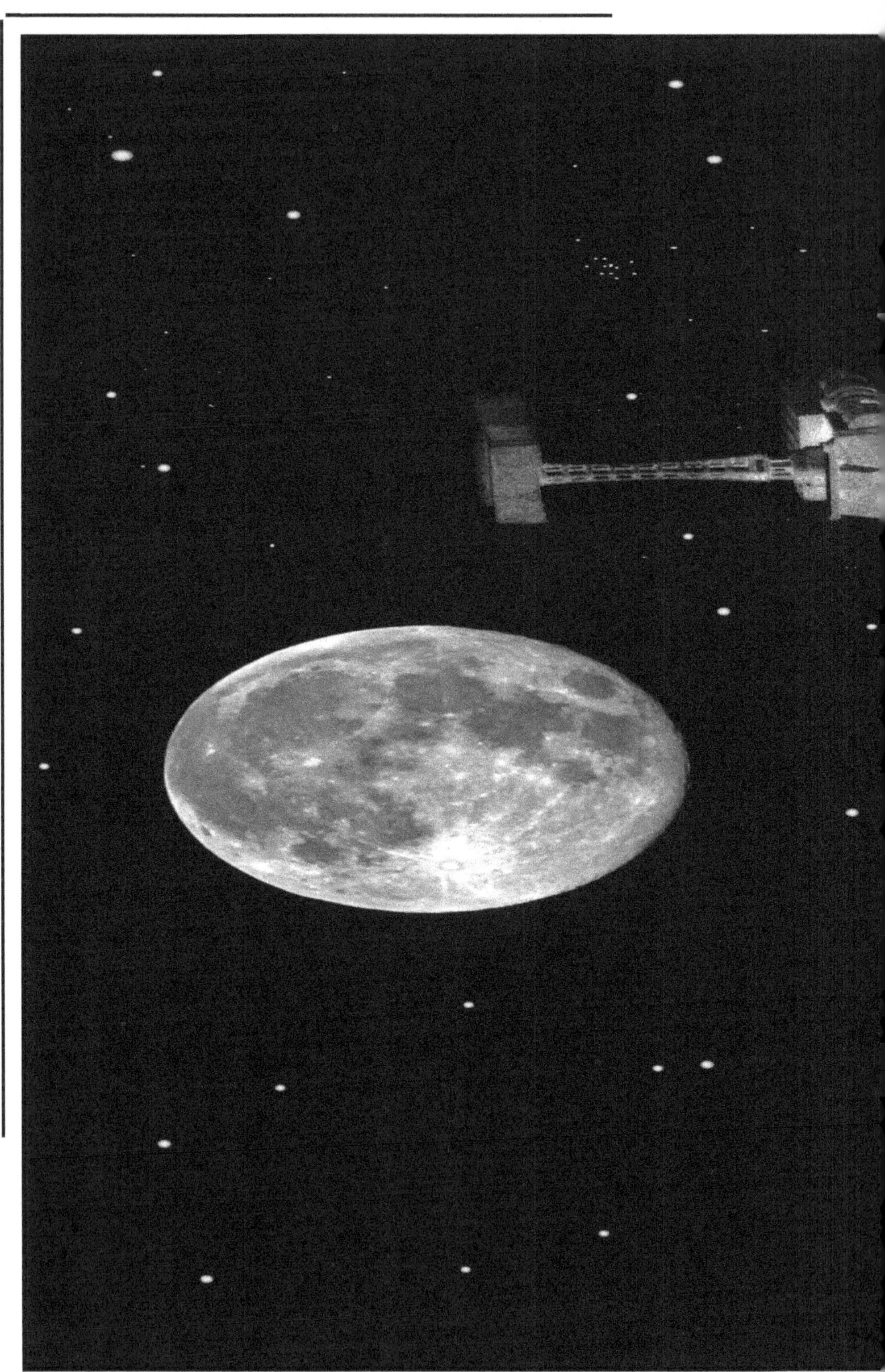

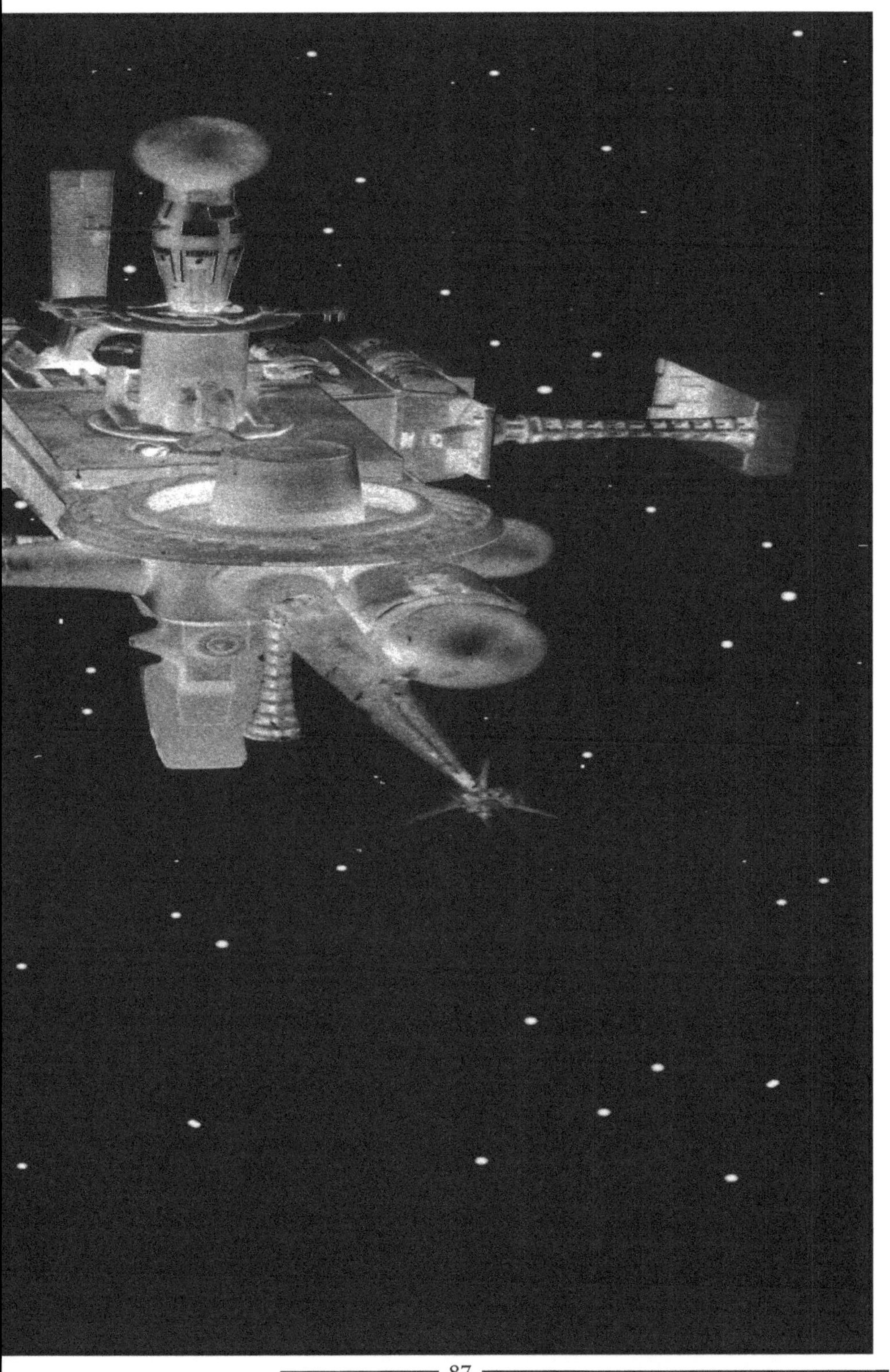

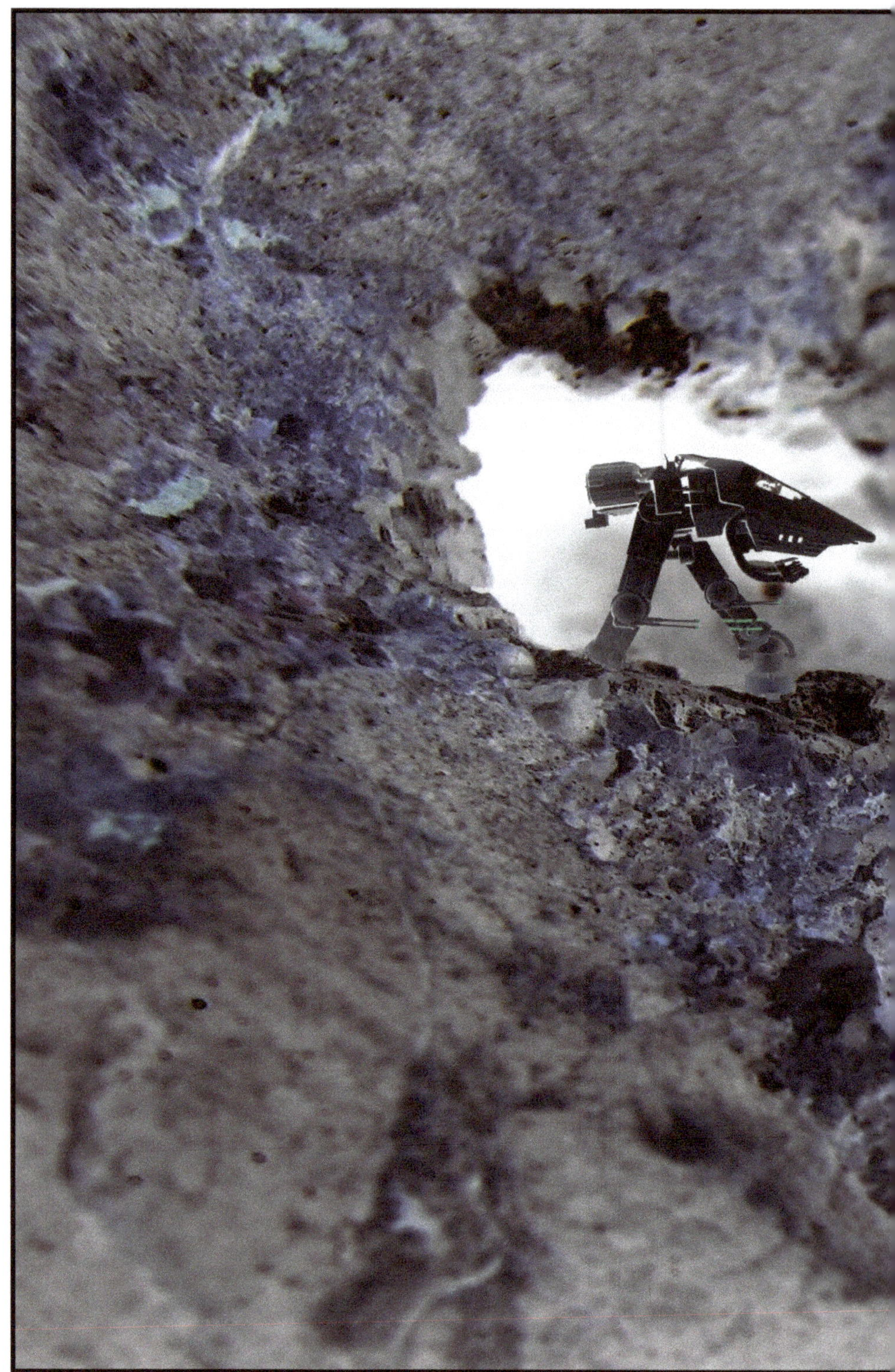

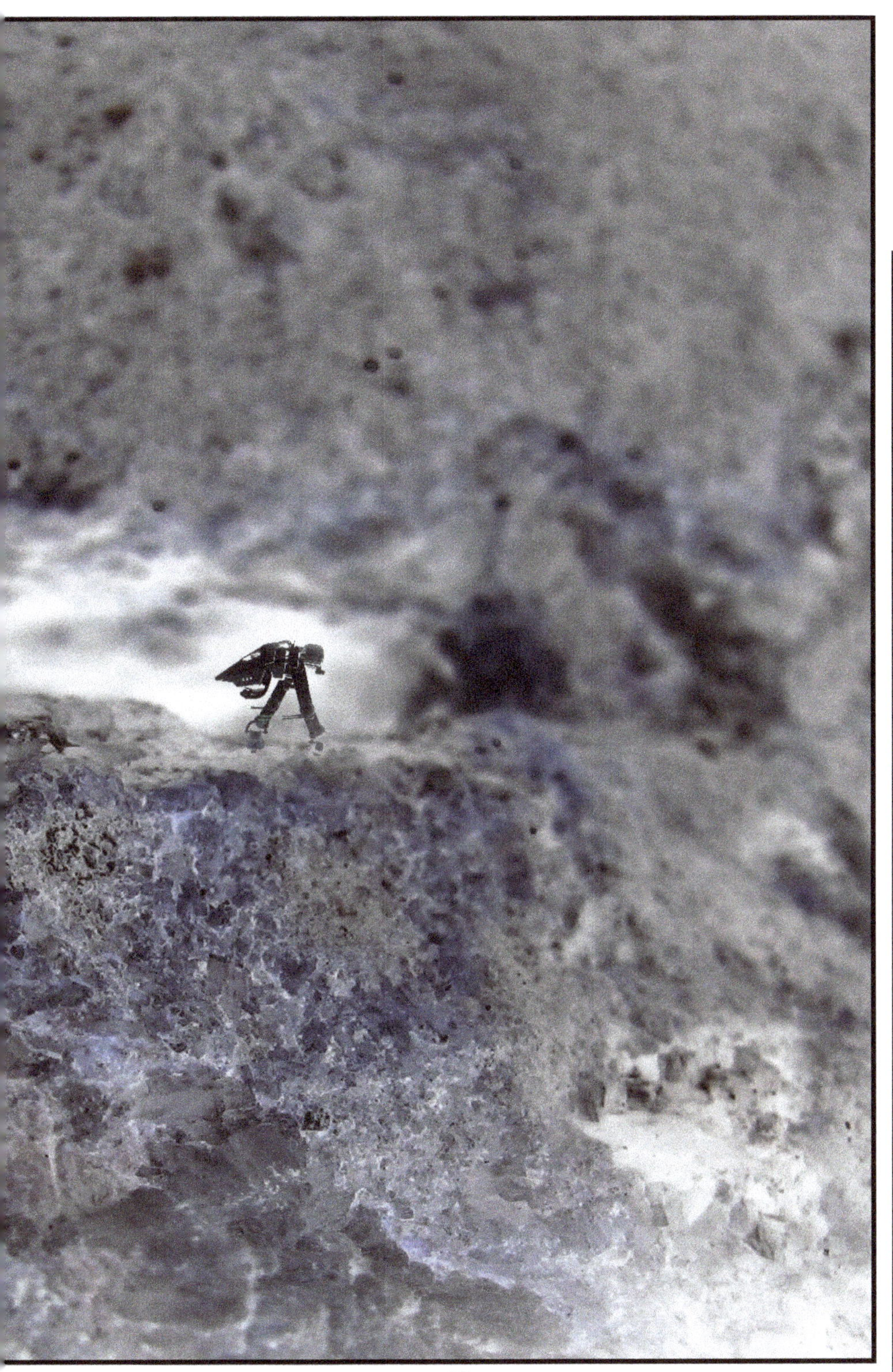

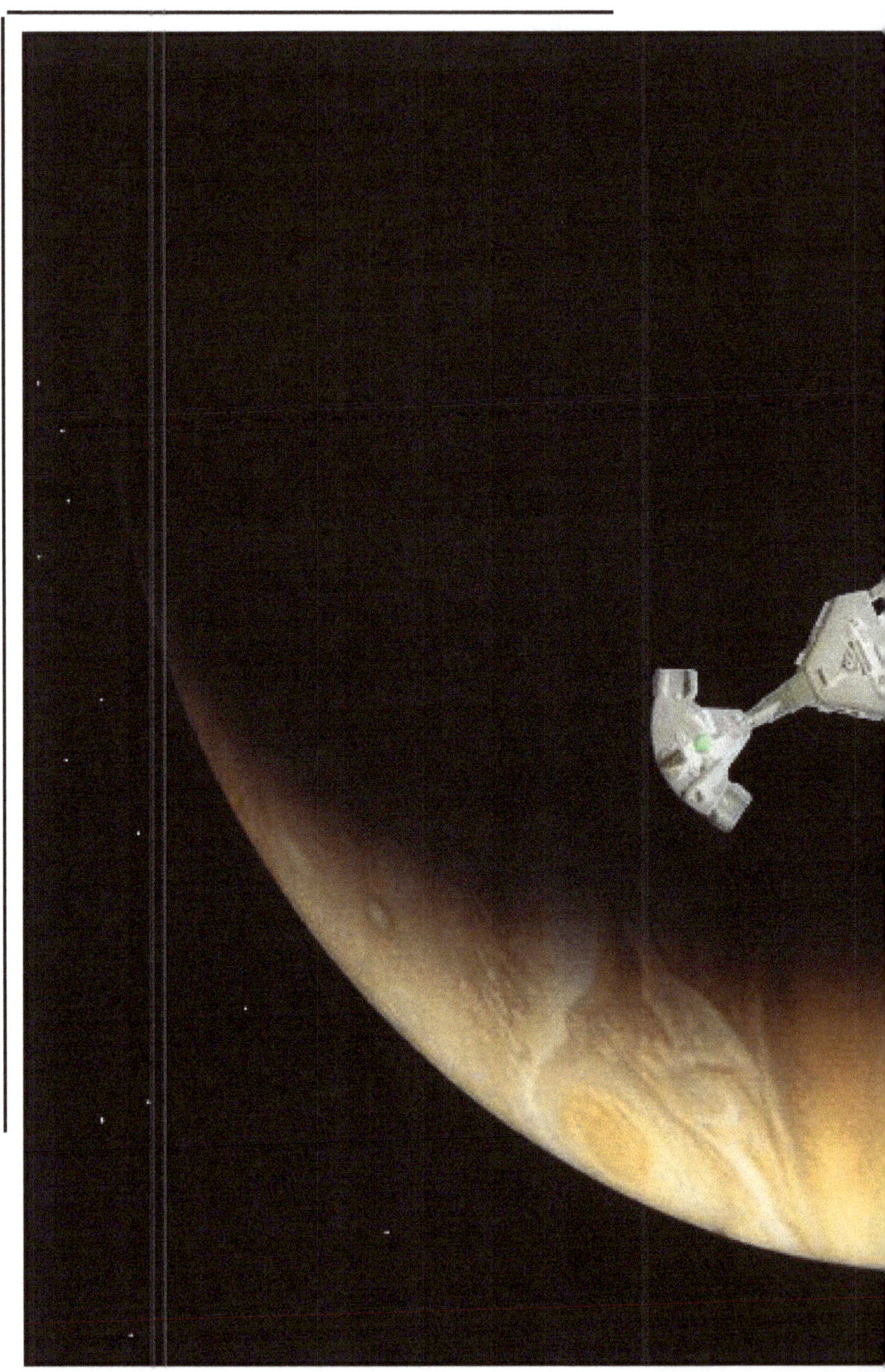

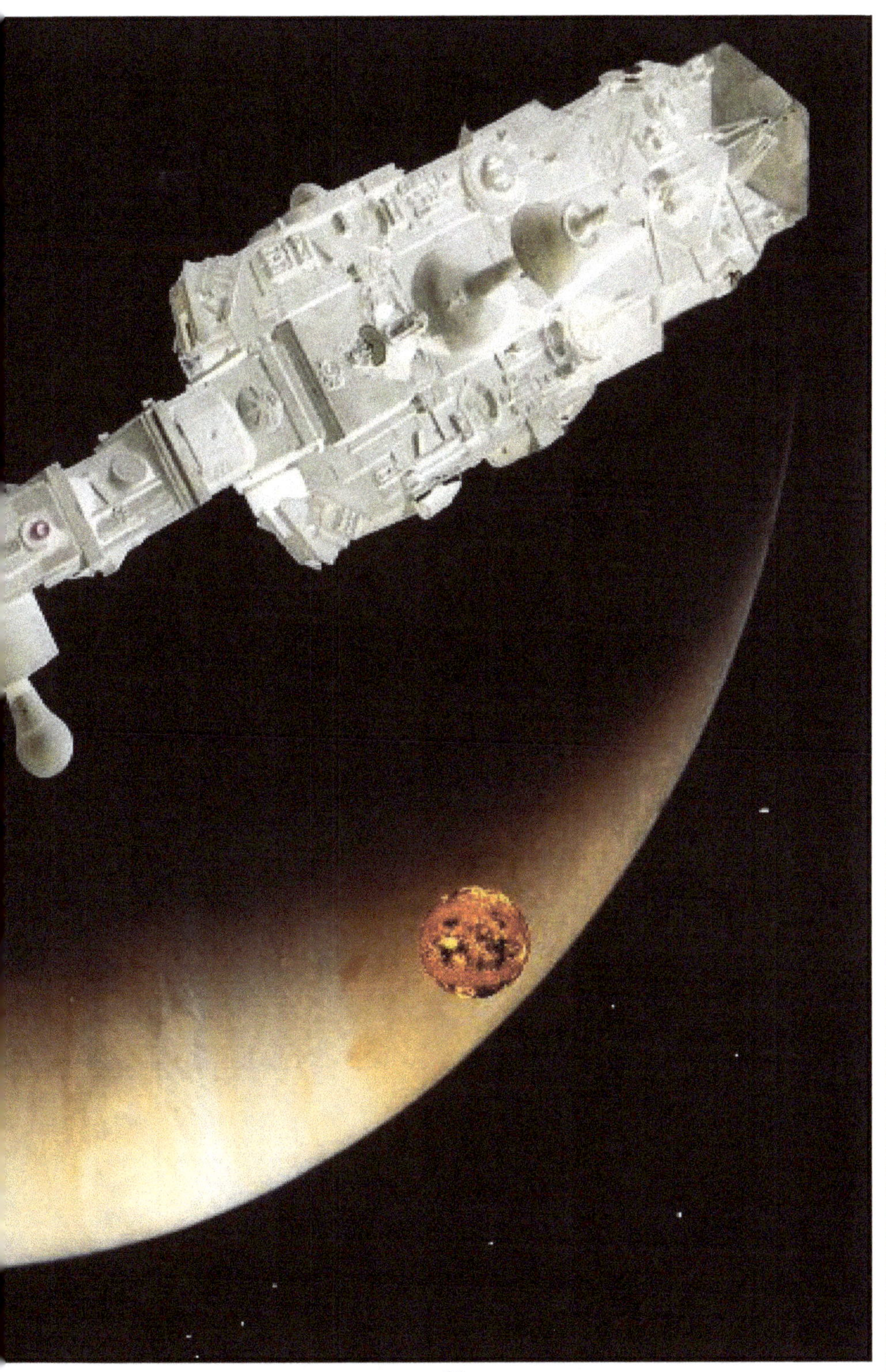

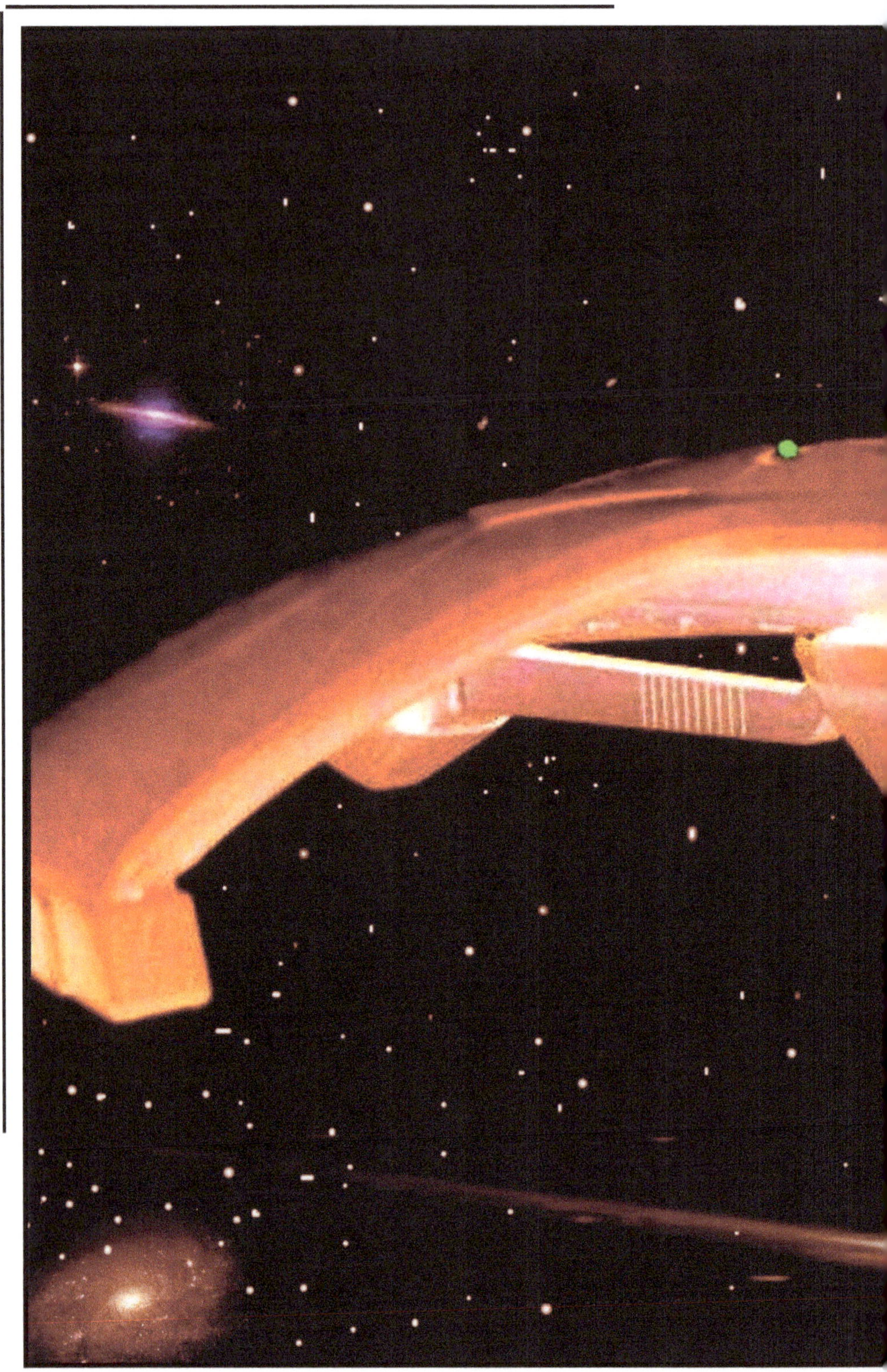

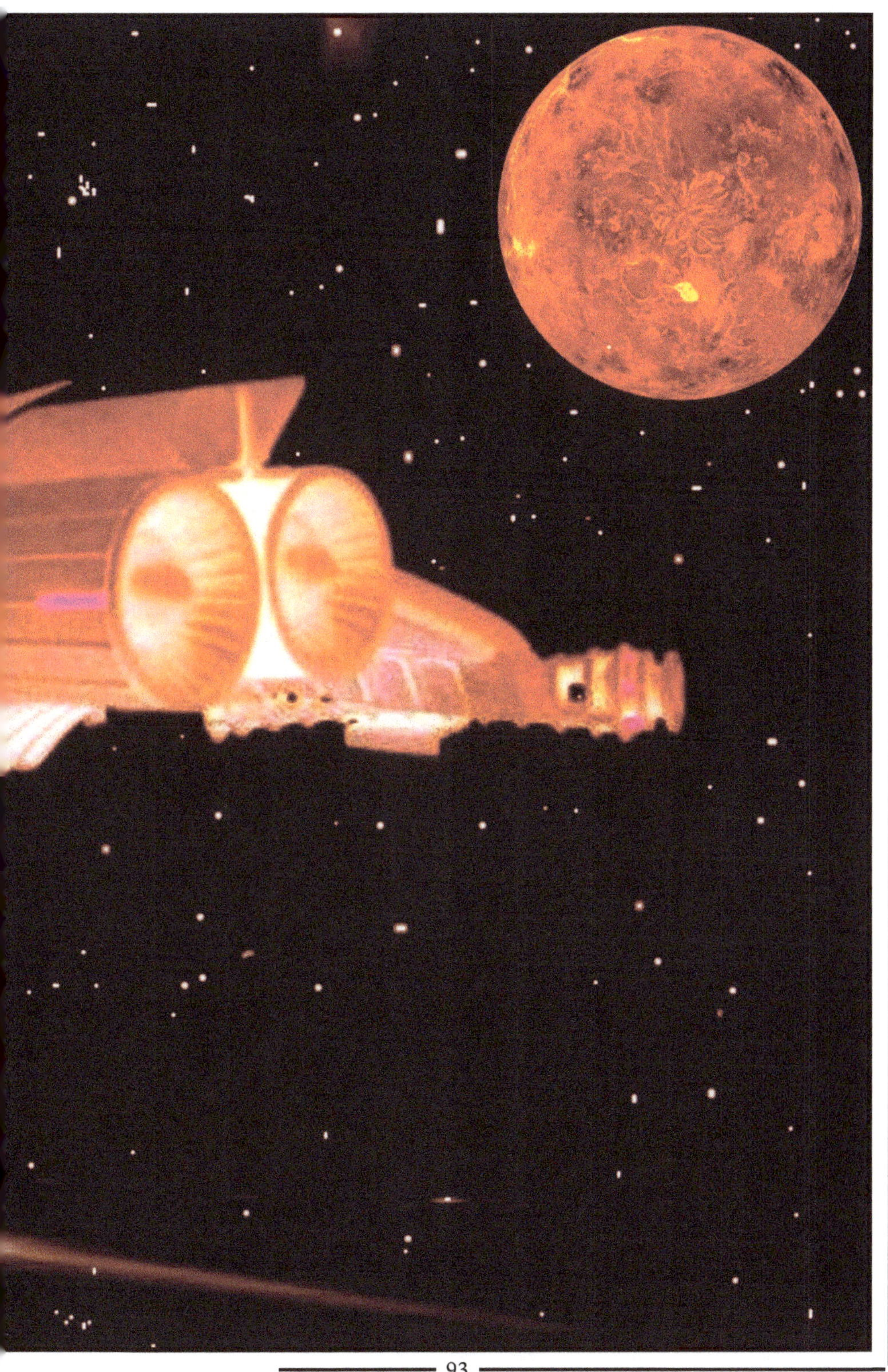

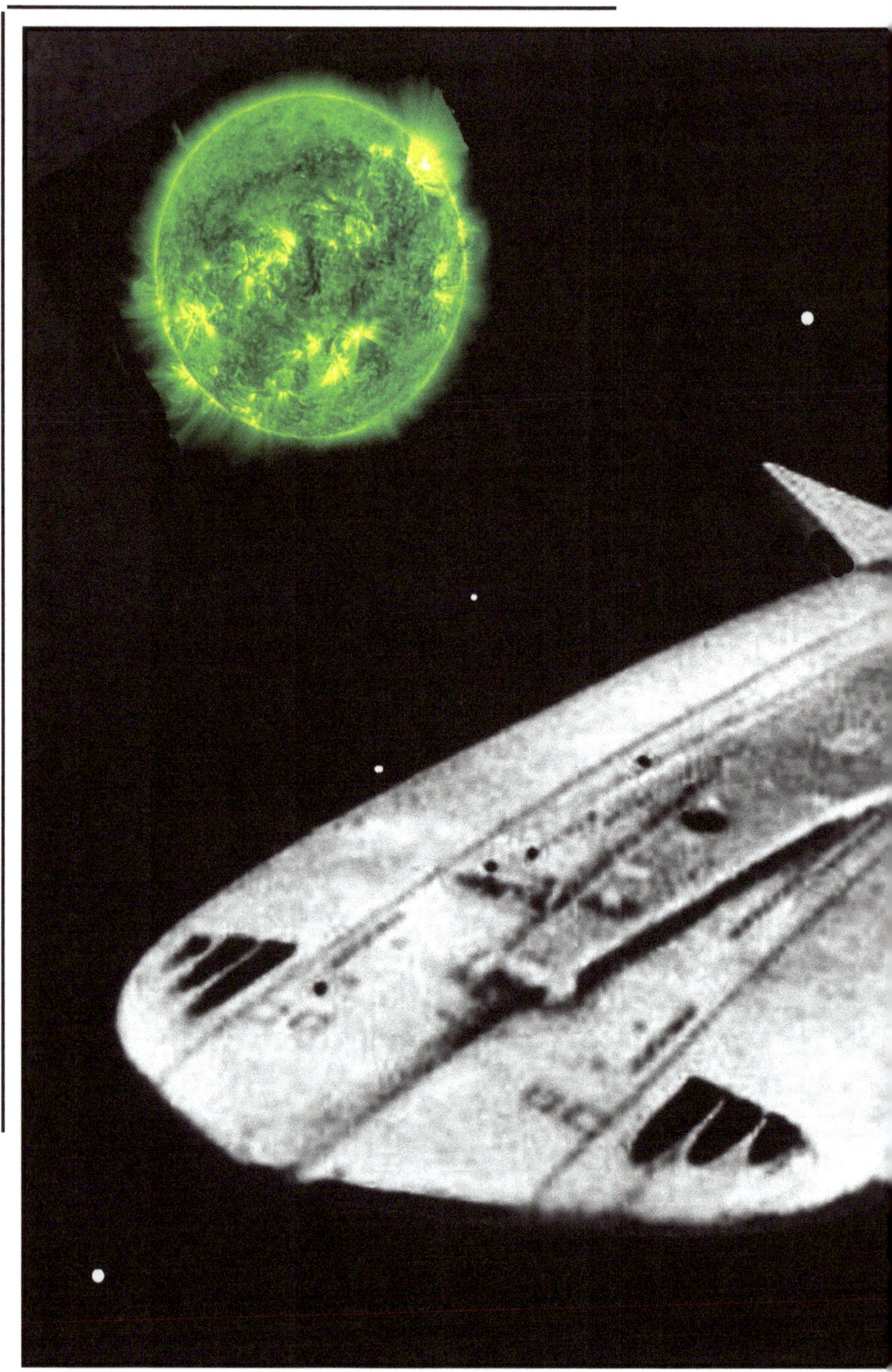

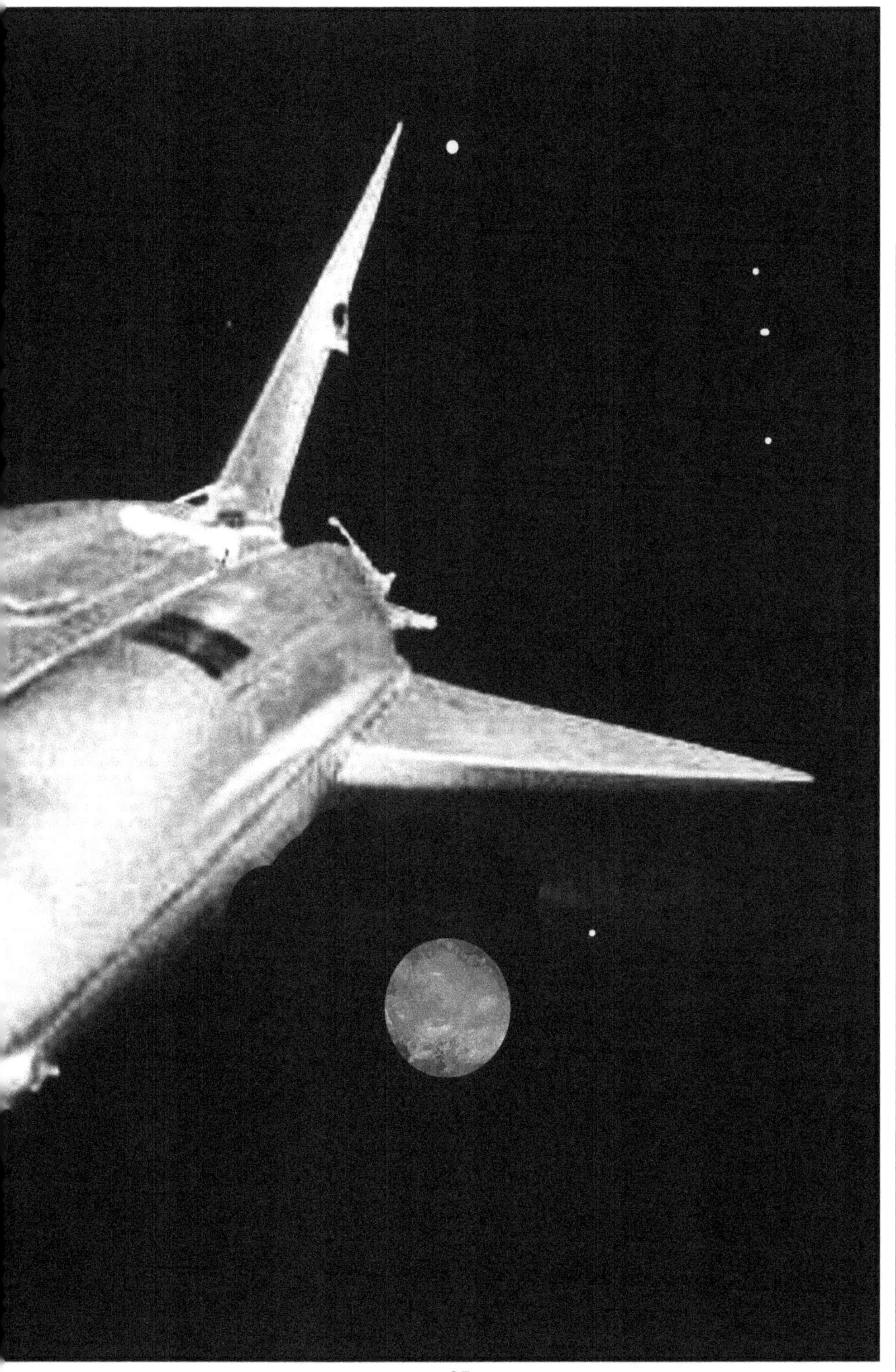

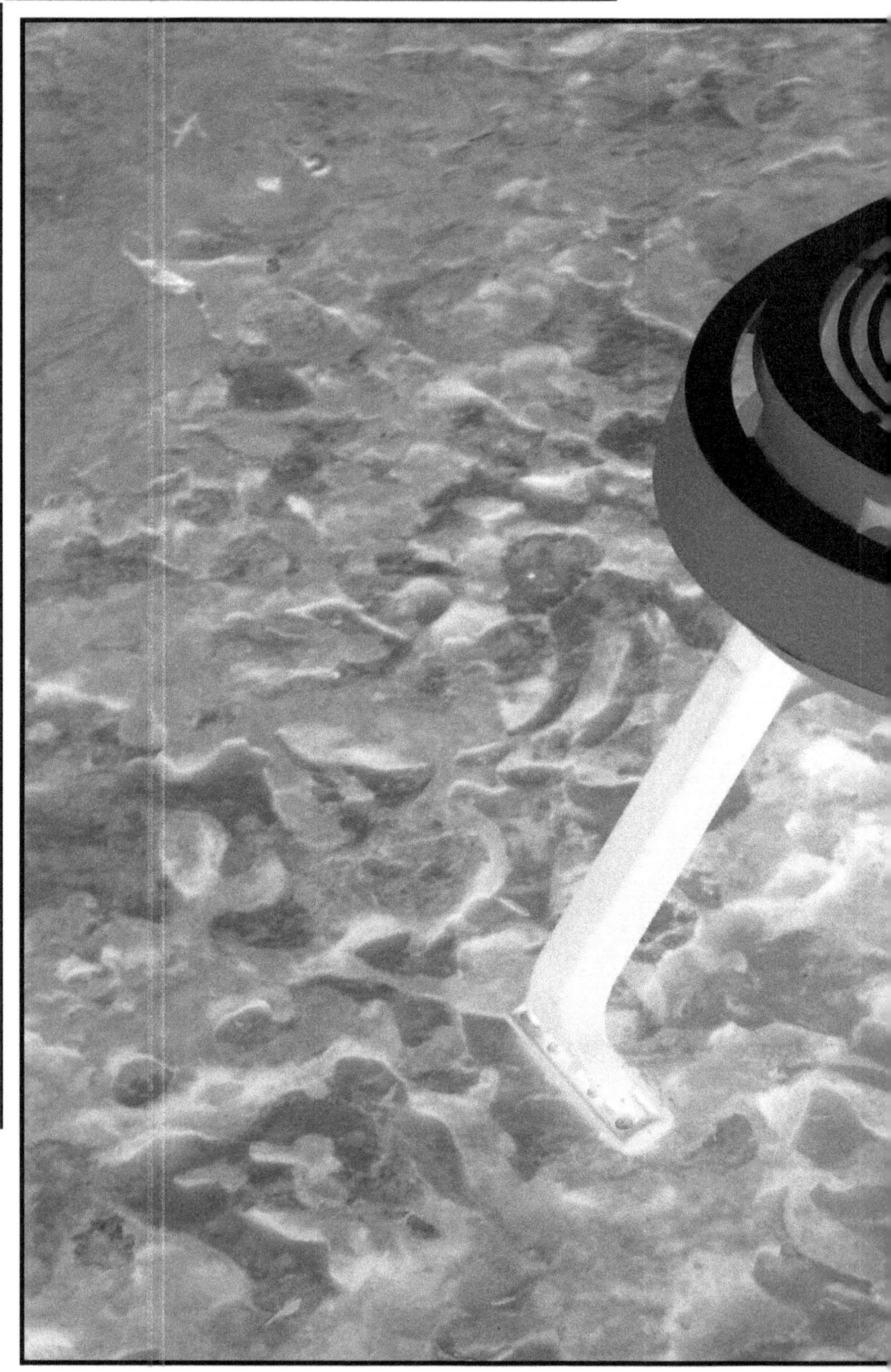

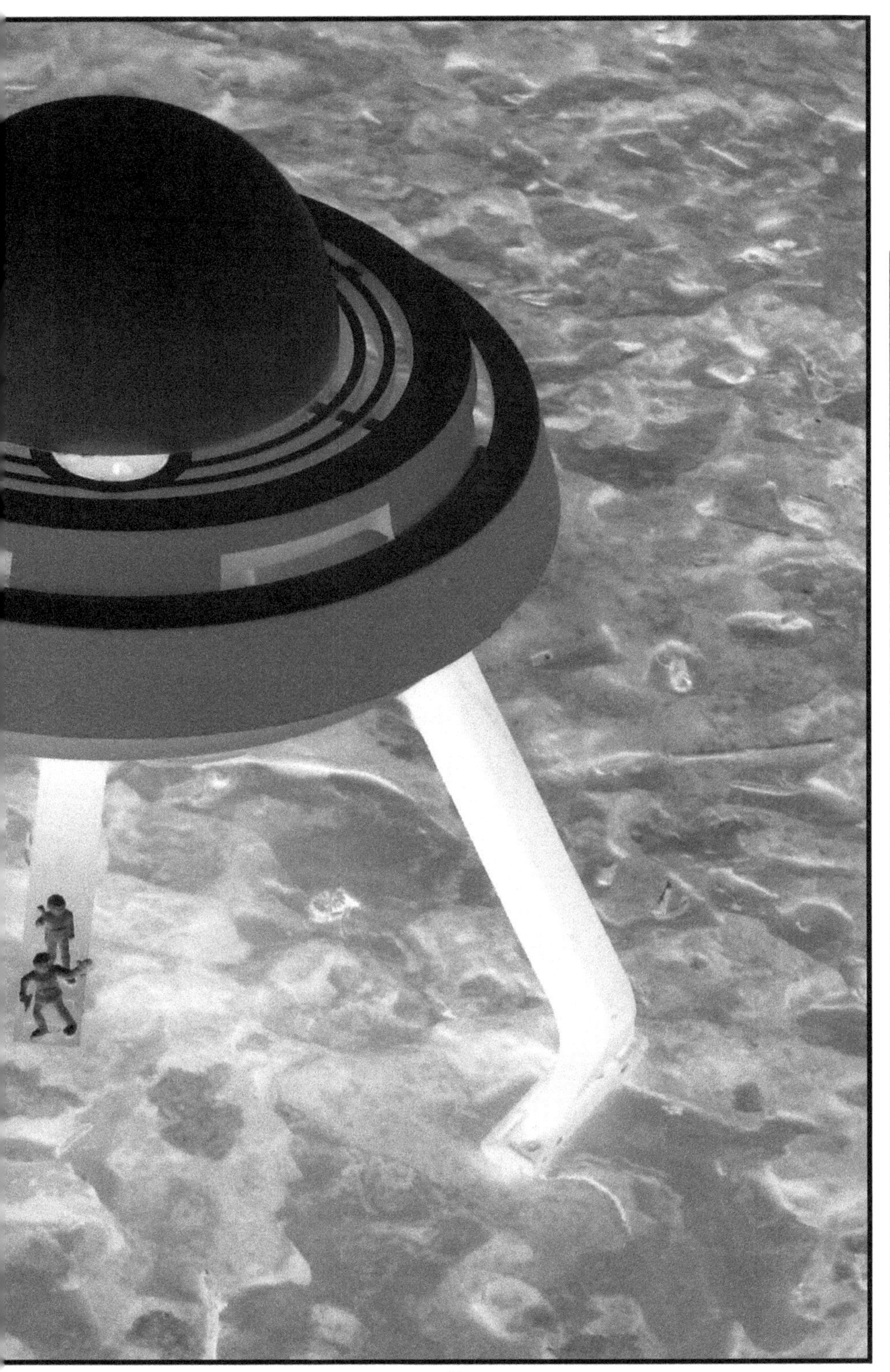

ILLEGIBLE

Avleen K Mokha

Bedroom floor lore says they spoke
long ago but never learned to read.
Uncombed they sat squat on trains,
dead already by mistake. In London

I heard a woman scream for the engine
in us. In Montreal I heard a man lose
his eyes on a walk to the park:

Dogged, minds shorn of hope,
they live out their lives mechanically.

The myth of disbelief sometimes
catches up to me. At least
they got, the illiterate lot,
a train for their dead-not-yet.

They give their bodies unprompted
to an illegible ache, pacify
the feeling that only takes.

All concurred the murders occurred,
but no one was there
to write it down.

Dolphins (a suicide note)

Jonathan Douglas Duran

"Impregnate a distant world"- That was the original pitch, and it spoke directly to the American male's manifest destiny fetish. Obviously, it sold very well... and why not- people were full of fear, consumed with panic. The world was collapsing in on itself; everything was depleted, destroyed, or dying. Children were not part of Earth's future they said; our seeds would wither and die within us. Yet instead of accepting responsibility, tempering our actions, taking control and fixing what we had damaged, we simply decided to alter our perspective. Literally... we aimed higher and set our sights to the sky.

The vast expanse of *space* was to be our national womb, our mistress to be used—celestial legs spread eternal wide, inviting us in. We will now force ourselves upon an infinite and unwitting cosmos. Thanks to the staggering scope of the military industrial complex and its generous corporate benefactors, we could now evolve into warheads—weaponize our DNA to rebuild the caustic force of mankind someplace new.

The program launched with a multi-billion-dollar marketing campaign. Celebrities and politicians waved to hungry crowds as they entered into the facility, being interviewed in their stunning gowns and sharp suits while the press licked boot and asked regurgitated themes on the same question ad nauseam: 'how does it feel to be so special?' The program even earned the full and hearty endorsement of the Church—the Pope himself crawled down off his golden throne to personally take part.

There were three packages offered in this 'intergalactic insemination' project. The first option was the cheapest and most popular, as it allowed you to hedge your bets—you could simply send your sperm into space while you stayed here to see how things played out. A small, personalized seed pod would carry your fluid out of our atmosphere and then essentially wander space. What's supposed to happen then is anyone's guess... the pamphlets become quite vague after they convince you it will be easy to ejaculate into a little cup. It's the concept, in the abstract, that sells this option—'Shoot your load into space.' Everyone signed up for the larger packages gets this option as a free add-on, however... women are only *encouraged to utilize any spermatozoa they prefer.'* Why they didn't just allow them to freeze their eggs and send those into orbit comes down to that age-old mentality of the capital, M-A-N being in control of all reproductive decisions. They didn't want an alien race impregnating a human egg and making some disgusting hybrid species... no, they demanded honest-to-goodness, hand-made, MAN-made sperm would be the only thing allowed to do any penetrating to make half-alien babies.

Option two, known colloquially as 'the popsicle,' was to be cryogenically frozen, wholesale, altogether just as you are, and put into a large pod. They launch that pod into open space and then it's up to fate. Perhaps, they tantalizingly taunt, in a

thousand years you'll awaken on a distant world to find yourself worshipped as a
God. However, the mathematical reality was that you would float forever and never
awaken, or worse, be pulled into a black hole and cease to ever exist in the first place.
This option was most attractive to the seniors; they figured they didn't have long left,
why not play the cosmic lottery and see if their luck panned out. Einstein famously
said, "God doesn't play dice", but then, Einstein didn't have the disposable income
that people have today, so how would he know. Besides, from what I've witnessed,
God is obviously a degenerate gambler.

Option three was reserved for the economic one-percenters since they were
the only folks who could afford it—otherwise it would take thirty plus years in one
of the high-paying labor camps to even come close to working it off. For a sum equal
that of a medium-sized nation's GDP, the premium package promised a full, mature
and cerebrally coherent clone. You continue to live however you see fit; meanwhile
you—*a copy of you*—goes into the pod, is fed intravenously, grows, and eventual-
ly, at whatever pre-determined age you request, the pod's engines engage and the
on-board guidance systems head toward the gravitational pull of the nearest planet.
When awakened your clone is presented with detailed instructions and video tutori-
als, they don the included space suit and step out onto an alien world, fully prepared
to colonize. The pod contains everything needed: an armory of guns, a year's supply
of fresh water and dehydrated food, a briefcase of seeds carefully curated by top
botanists, and all the equipment necessary to set up a small hydroponic lab. The pod
itself doubles as a shelter and you're even afforded fifty terabytes of films, music and
e-books to entertain, distract and relax with. They made it seem like they thought of
everything, and maybe they really did.

It became the main event of our wheezing culture: millions of people, lining
up around the storefronts for weeks to gladly pay the exorbitant costs with big, dumb
smiles plastered across their mugs. This was the next big thing, possibly *the last big
thing*—you don't want to be left behind. It was genius; the perfect, unholy marriage of
our consumerist lust and our solipsistic dreams of immortality. The future of death
turned out to be just another way for the cynical present to continue unabated into
a for-profit afterlife. You see, marketing had become the dominant religion without
anyone realizing it. We worshipped at invisible altars all around us, on every screen,
billboard, and shiny new product designed to deliver adverts to us twenty-four hours
a day. We were tracked and recorded and quantified, then barraged with exactly
what we wanted before we knew we wanted it. The desires were manufactured, and
they bred marketing campaigns inside of us, then, believing it to be our own taste,
we evangelized the gospel outward, made it part of our self-perceptions. Our brands
defined us, useful idiot cultists that we were. People starved in the streets, children
lived in cages, and yet everyone kept buying nine hundred-dollar cellphones for rea-
sons they didn't understand. This is how it all worked: goods, services, politics, the
tax code. A contrived economic servitude we all ached to take part in, for fear that we
may miss out on a grand, nebulous *something*.

Me on the other hand... I'm disgusted by the lot of it. The idea that we are willing to send our madness out into the universe is too much for me to abide. We will eat up all of outer space if given the chance. No place will ever be safe from our insatiable hunger for domain. Of this, I am certain.

For those who think this is hyperbole, if you're unfamiliar, let me just tell you—our history was not kind. The insidious truth was there existed a concerted, prolonged effort to manufacture and cultivate hatred on a scale previously unthinkable. We took and raped and killed and lied and demonized our fellow man over trivialities so we could tell ourselves we were 'better' than them. We did whatever we damn well pleased and called anyone else scum who even attempted to take us to task for our actions or rhetoric. We allowed ourselves to be demeaned, our spirits bound, our minds depressed, our grotesqueries overfed. We lost sight of our potential and were tricked into the idea of working and paying and ignoring our true selves while busily celebrating the wolves in sheep's clothes gnawing away at our guts. We sold our human potential down the river to continuously line the pockets of a handful of unimaginative bureaucrats because they scared our benumbed limbic brains into thinking they were our only salvation, our only path to safety and stability. We were to blame, we, the willfully ignorant. Of all evils foisted upon us from every direction, our sickening passivity and cowardice was the most intolerable since it was entirely within our power to change. Really, that was our only power, and nobody used it. No one tried to stop anything and by the time we realized how dire things really were, it was too late anyway.

Which is how I've come to this... one thing I ask you to remember is that humans, by and large, had a long history of revolution. But revolution can be quiet and internal, just as often (if not more so) as it can be raucous and bloody.

Rumor is, somewhere out there in the brown muck that was once pristine blue ocean, a few places still supported life in a somewhat normal fashion. I'd been told on good authority there is such a place where, believe it or not, dolphins still lived. They swim and squeak and you can walk right up to them and touch them if you want, and after weeks of slow, dangerous travel through the blisteringly hot and drought-ravaged southern United States, I've finally made it here to see for myself. Signs still hang, announcing the opportunity to swim with 'therapy' dolphins. This was one of those places were the old, the infirm, and the enfeebled would come, wade out into a little area and be able to pet and interact with the dolphins in their 'natural habitat.' I know it seems silly... *dolphins*... who cares, right? I don't know much about the creatures and I have no strong affinity for them one way or another... but outside of a few thousand dogs and cats, most animal life died off long ago. I can't even tell you how long it's been since I've seen an actual, live animal that doesn't scurry on the ground and have antennae. Over the years, as things fell apart, I became more and more wistful, and began to obsessively think about running with a pack of wolves, flying in a purposeful 'V' with a flock of geese, bedding down on a pile of leaves with a family of deer... becoming part of nature, something larger and outside of humanity.

The idea that these particular dolphins were once therapy animals is extra comforting to me, un-ironically enough, because I do feel weary... I feel enfeebled. If there's somewhere to give yourself over to something compassionate and be healed, even in some small way, I need to embrace it. I need something non-human that's not inhuman. I need to know that once, *at least once*, there was some form of purity out there, something that made sense and was balanced, necessary, and wise in a way that we could never truly understand or emulate due to our sordid human nature, but all the same *was there* and for the shortest blip of time, even dominated this world.

The water isn't brown, but it's definitely not blue per se... more a slimy, oil-slicked-rainbow hue. But wouldn't you know it, it's true. Here they are: three goddamned living, breathing dolphins. Their skin looks a bit irritated, puffy and varnished with a gray pallor that doesn't seem a healthy, natural dolphin-gray... but otherwise, they seem fine, calm, and unconcerned. I walk toward them, and they pensively cut through the water around me, bobbing their heads up and down, taking stock, trying to determine if I am a threat. One of them brushes against my leg and barrel rolls in front of me a few times, its belly remains upward, and I stroke it gently. I hear a chitter, a few chirps and now I'm surround by the three of them, rubbing up against me like dogs, asking to be pet. With both my hands in the water, sliding over their slick skins I start to cry. So what, I start to fucking *sob*.

The whole scene reminds me of one of those classical novels of tragic romanticism where the young lovers, shunned by society for their scandalous love, walk hand in hand into the crashing waves, never to be seen again, preferring to die with one another on their own terms than to prostitute themselves to a world they didn't fit into. I notice small, malformed fish swimming around my feet; there's still a whole world thriving down below, I muse. I grab the dolphin's fin like a hand, and it guides me deeper, further out and I'm in up to my waist when I notice my skin tingling, a burning sensation from whatever chemicals I'm bathing in. I go further, until my feet lose purchase with the ground. When I'm up to my neck, I let go. I clamp my eyes shut and drift down slowly. Further and further down, with no intention of coming back up. I choose to revolt instead of going forward, instead of going upward. I choose rebellion on my own terms in this endless depth.

It's comforting, to know you have no real control, yet you can sometimes still command the internal chaos in small, delicate intervals. I proclaim agency and I choose to return where this whole mess began: our collective primordial womb, where we made our first grand mistake of slithering out of the muck—our true original sin. I give in to the pressure of fathoms, squeezing air from my lungs, swaddling me tightly for the return to our birthplace. The dolphins have left me and I'm alone, drifting in the mute darkness of subaqueous sensory nullification. My skin burns and itches and it feels like gasoline is seeping into every cut and crack and crease. I keep my eyes shut tight and envision my traumatic descension as evolutionary necessity. The deeper I go the darker and colder it gets, and I can't help but think of all those bodies floating through space, desperate to wake up and conquer anew. I think about the grand poverty of such a desire. I think of those suckers floating through space and I imagine a Red Giant, collecting them at the end of the universe like a cremation oven, burning them up with incomprehensibly dispassionate ferocity. A universe imbued with ironic justice is a marvelous dream. I think of everything swallowed up and voided out, I imagine the abolition of all forms of slavery, a future for the innocent. I trick myself into being hopeful one last time as I run out of oxygen.

Invisible Nature

Marieken Cochius

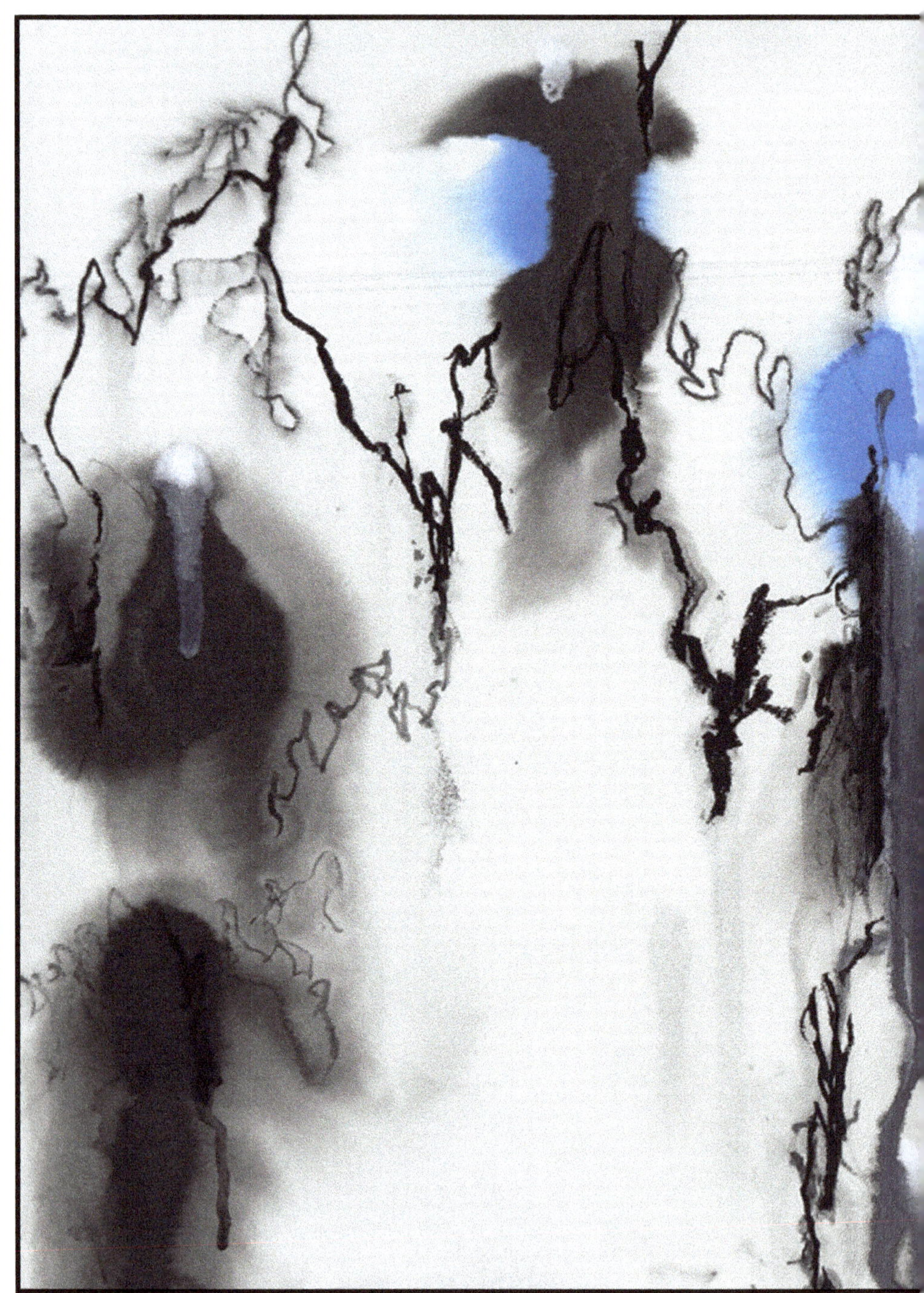

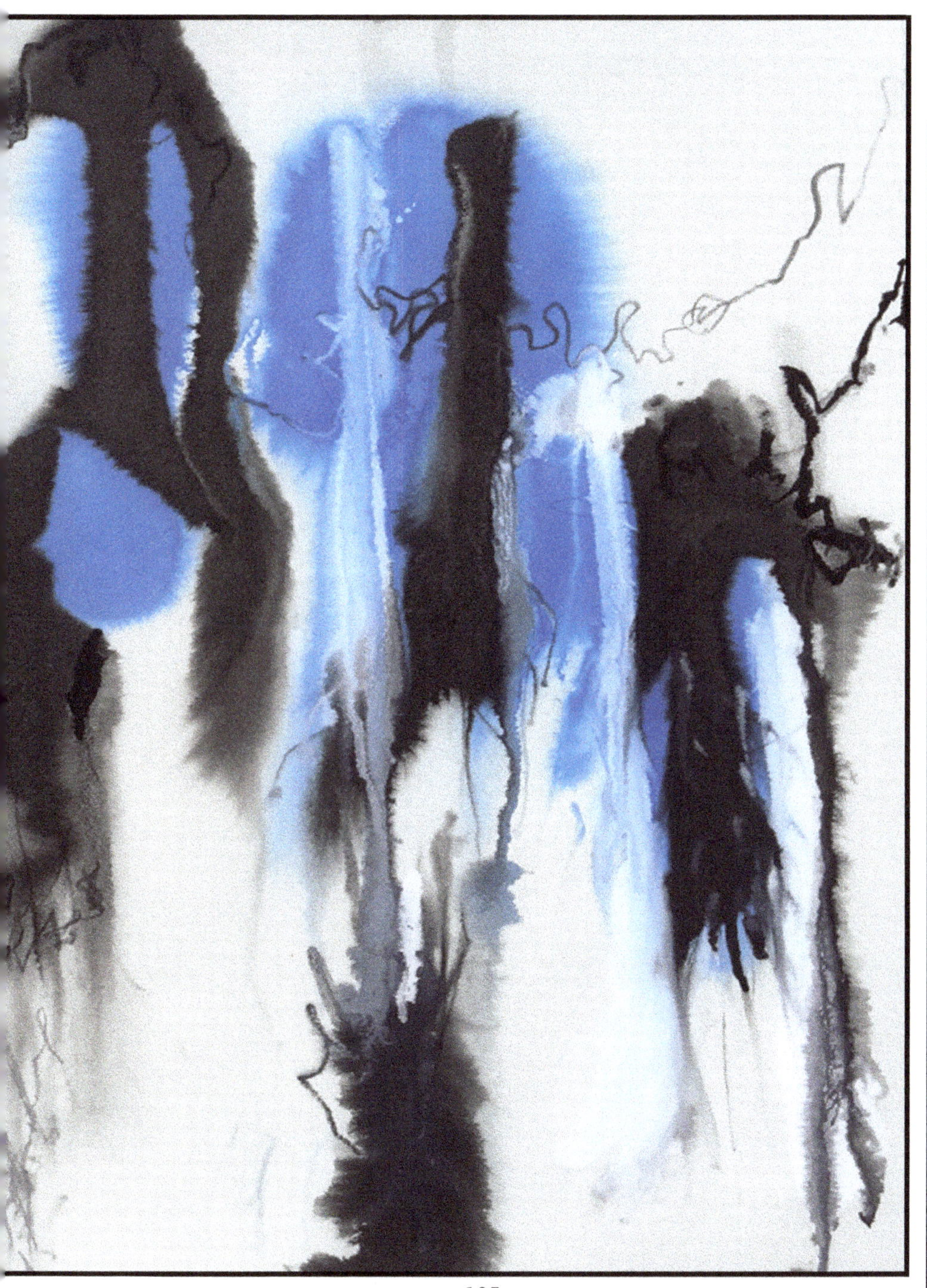

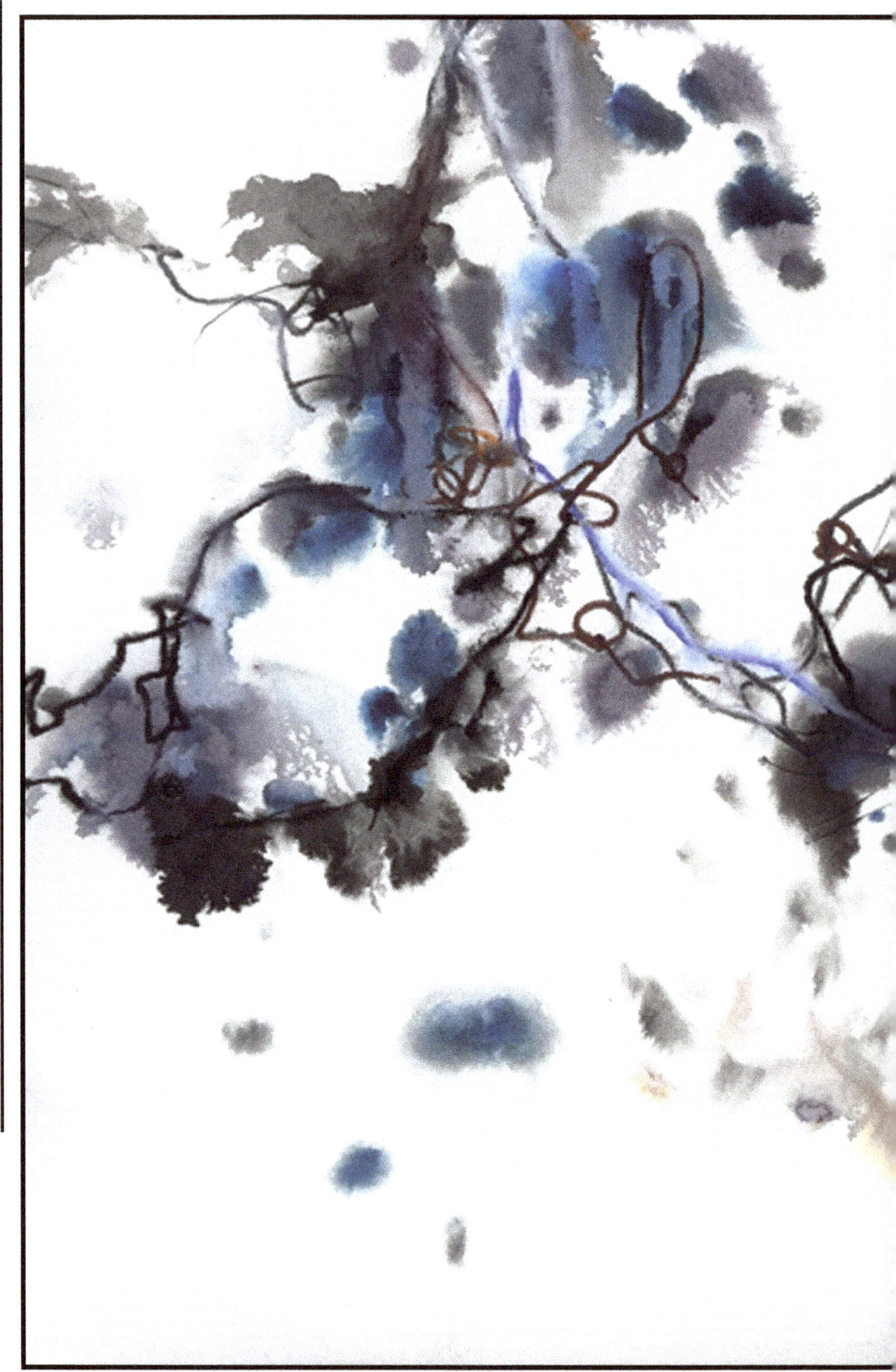

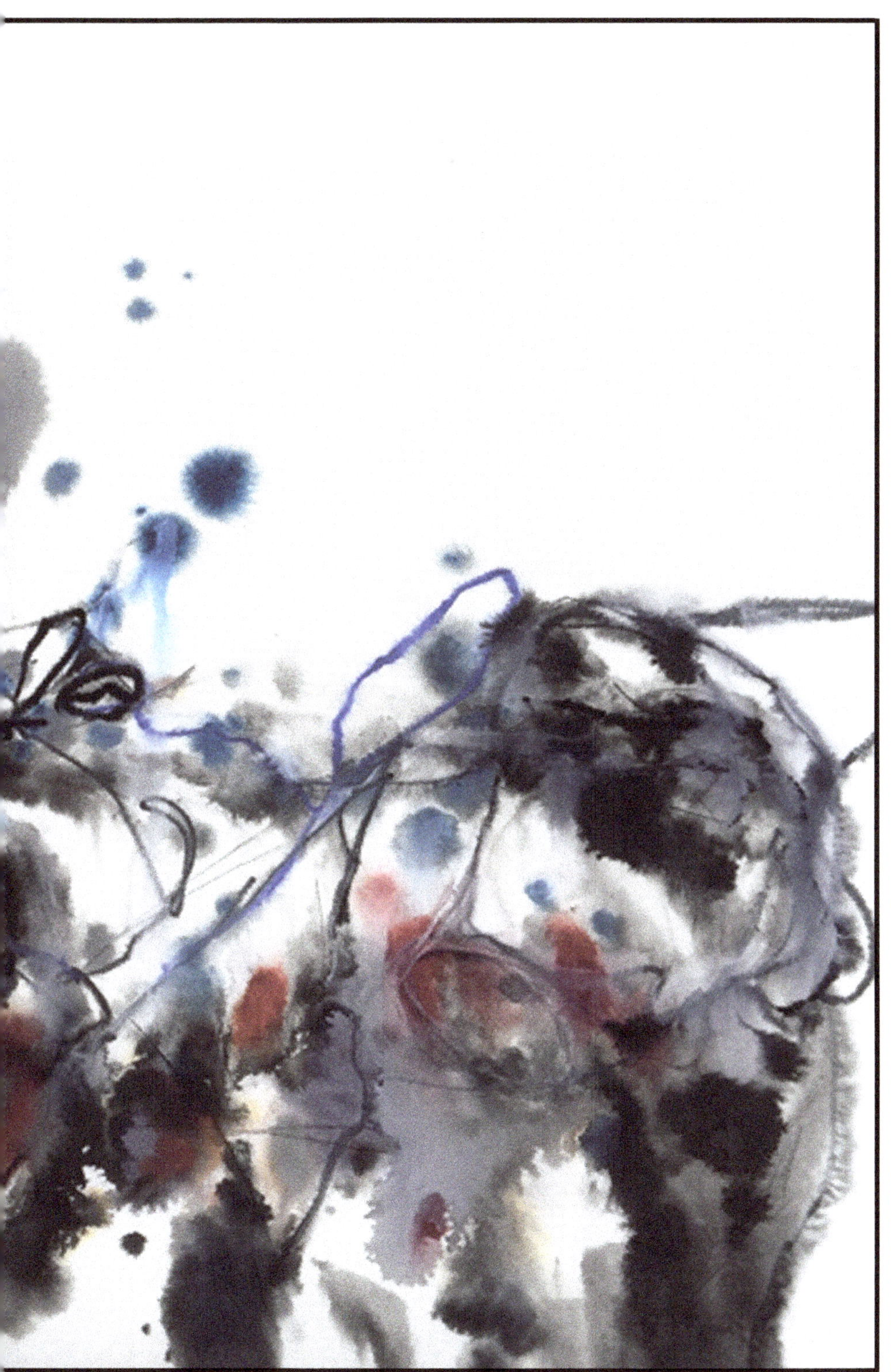

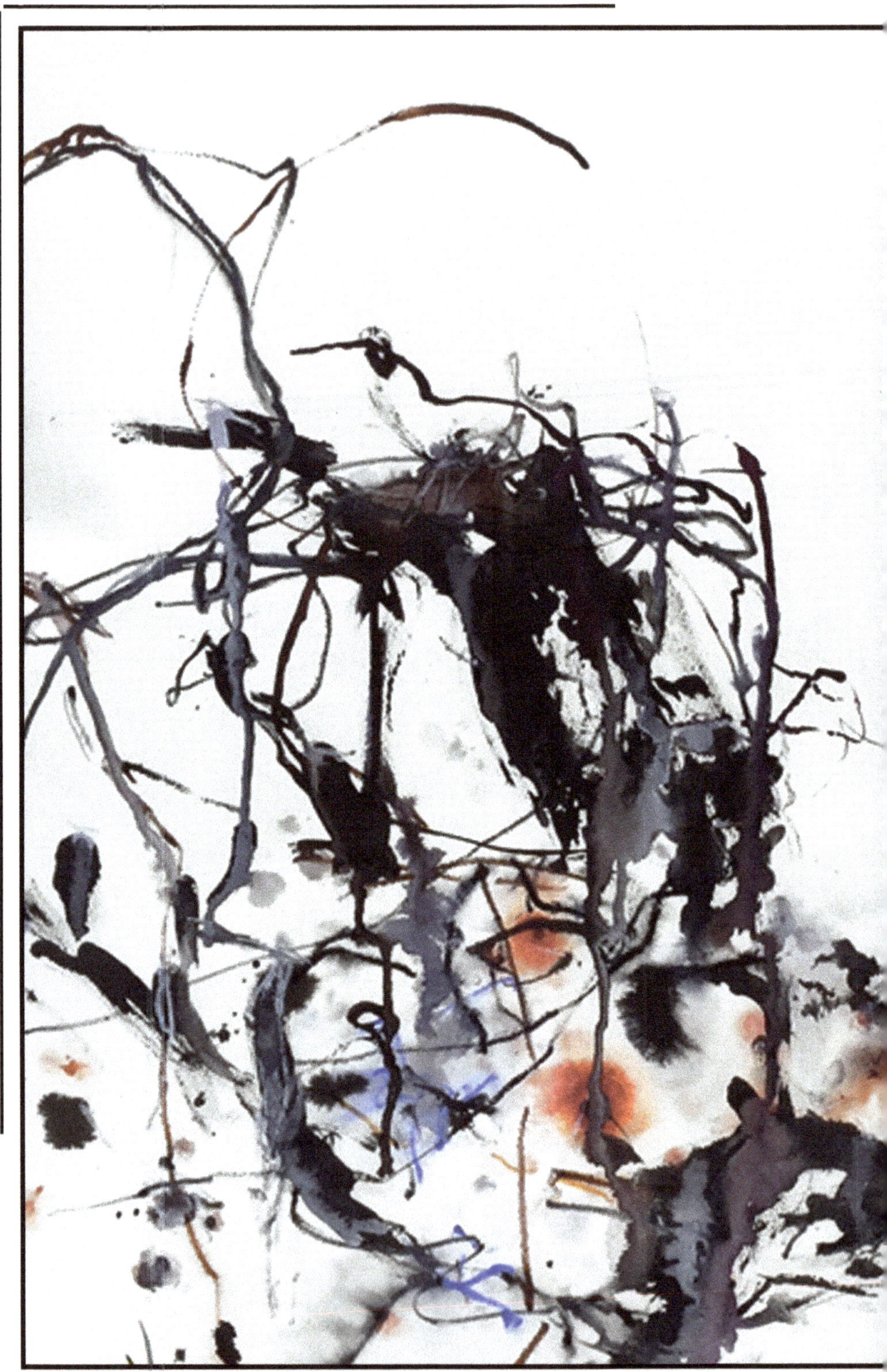

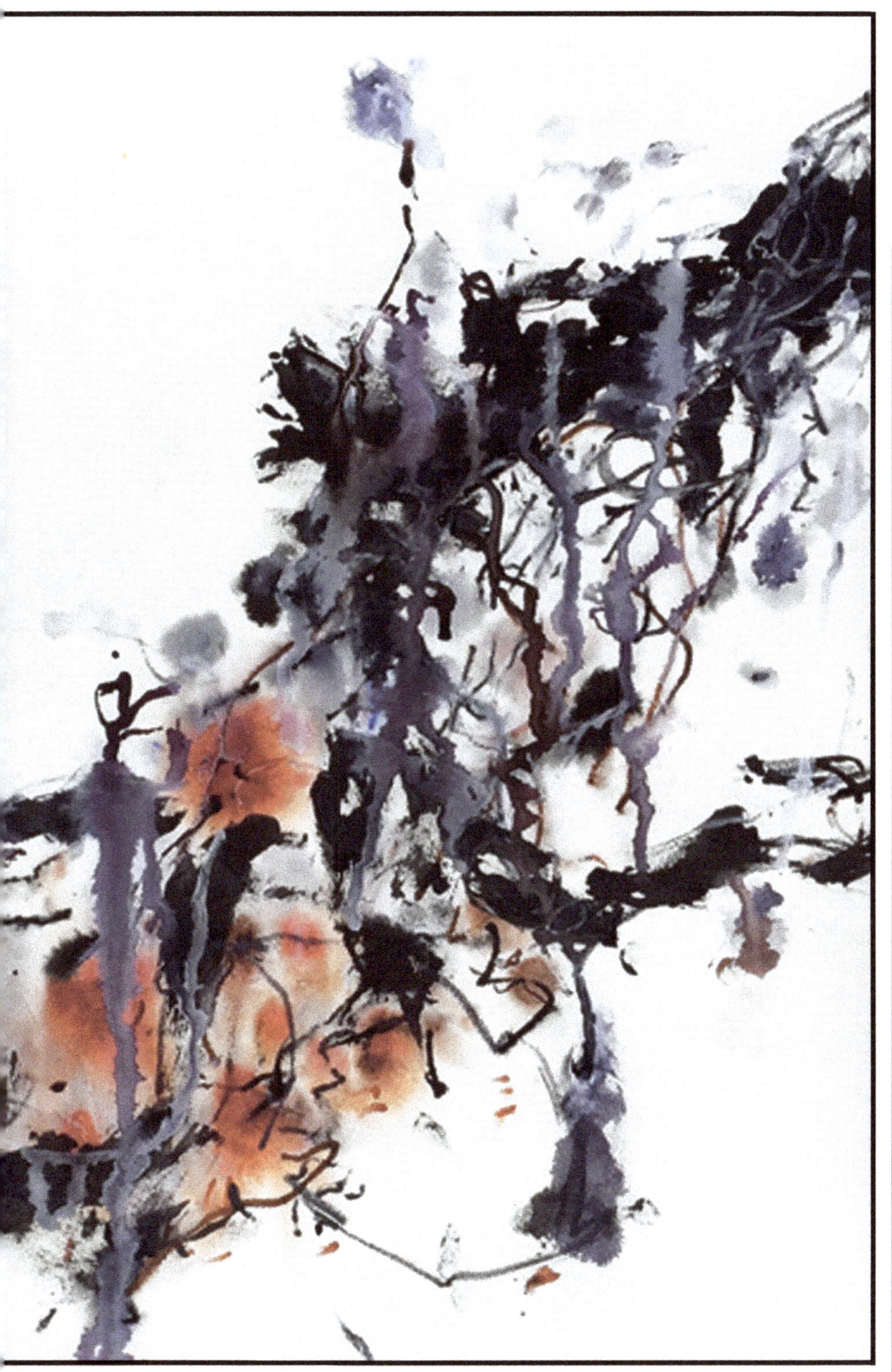

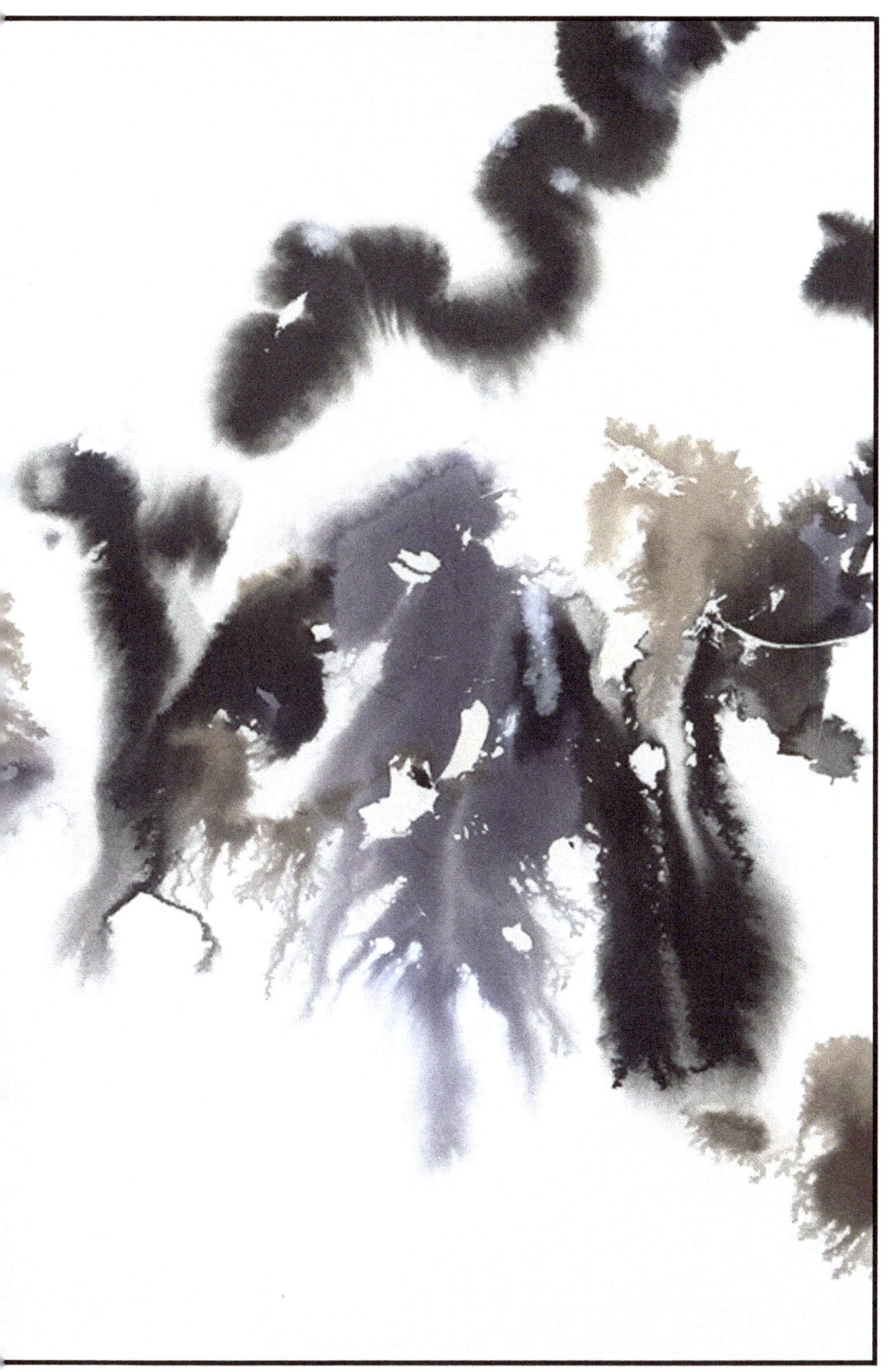

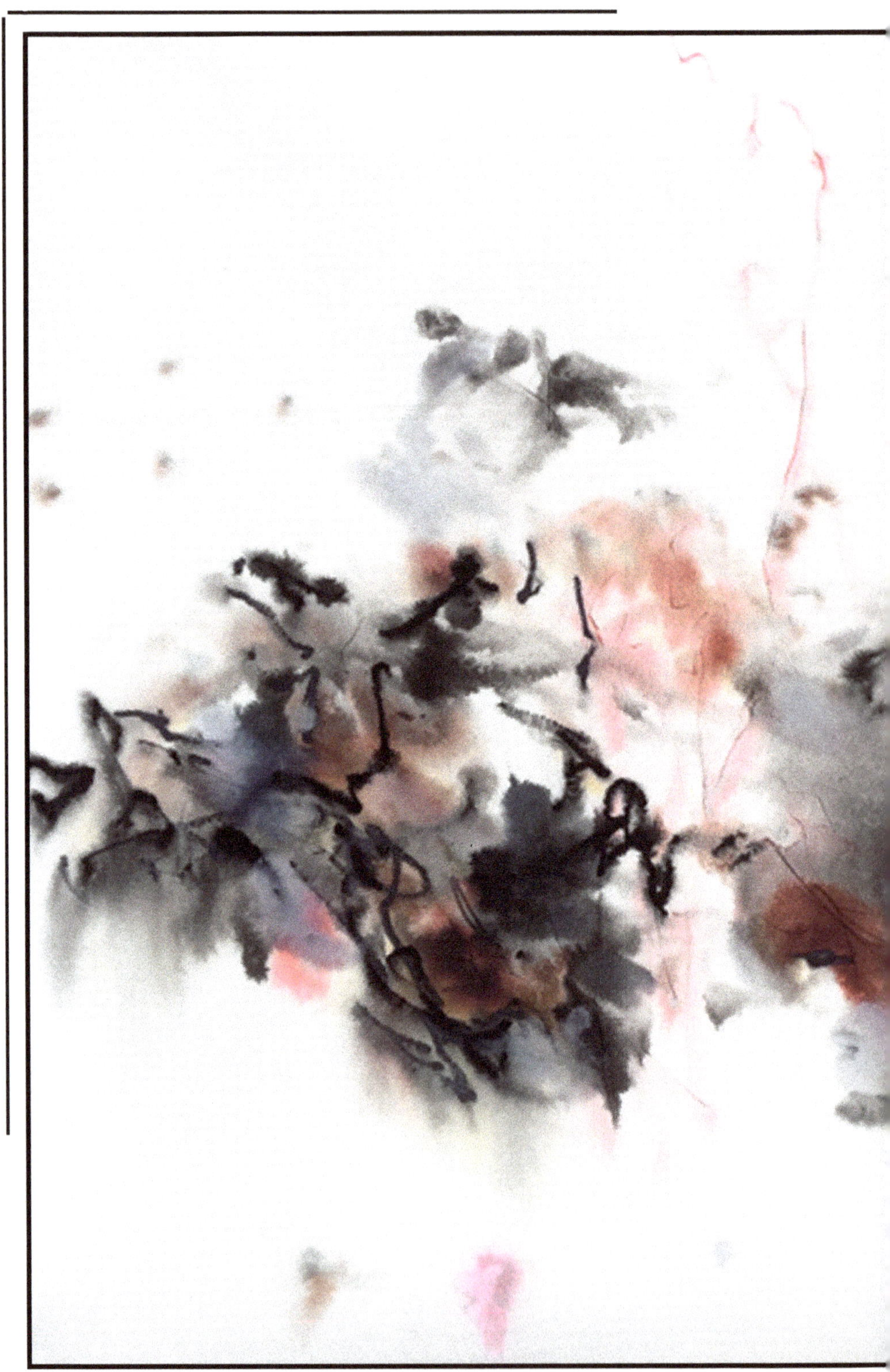

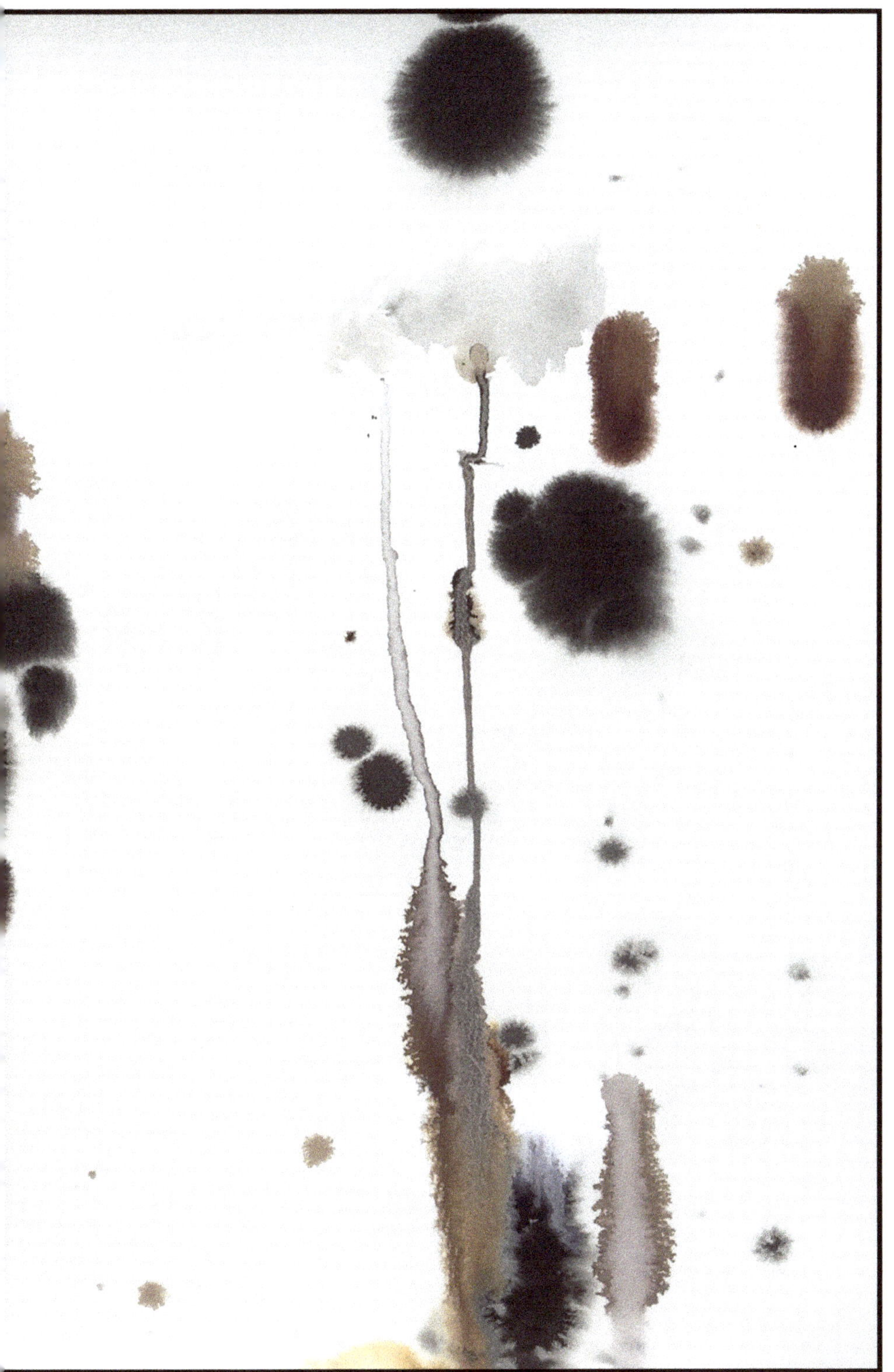

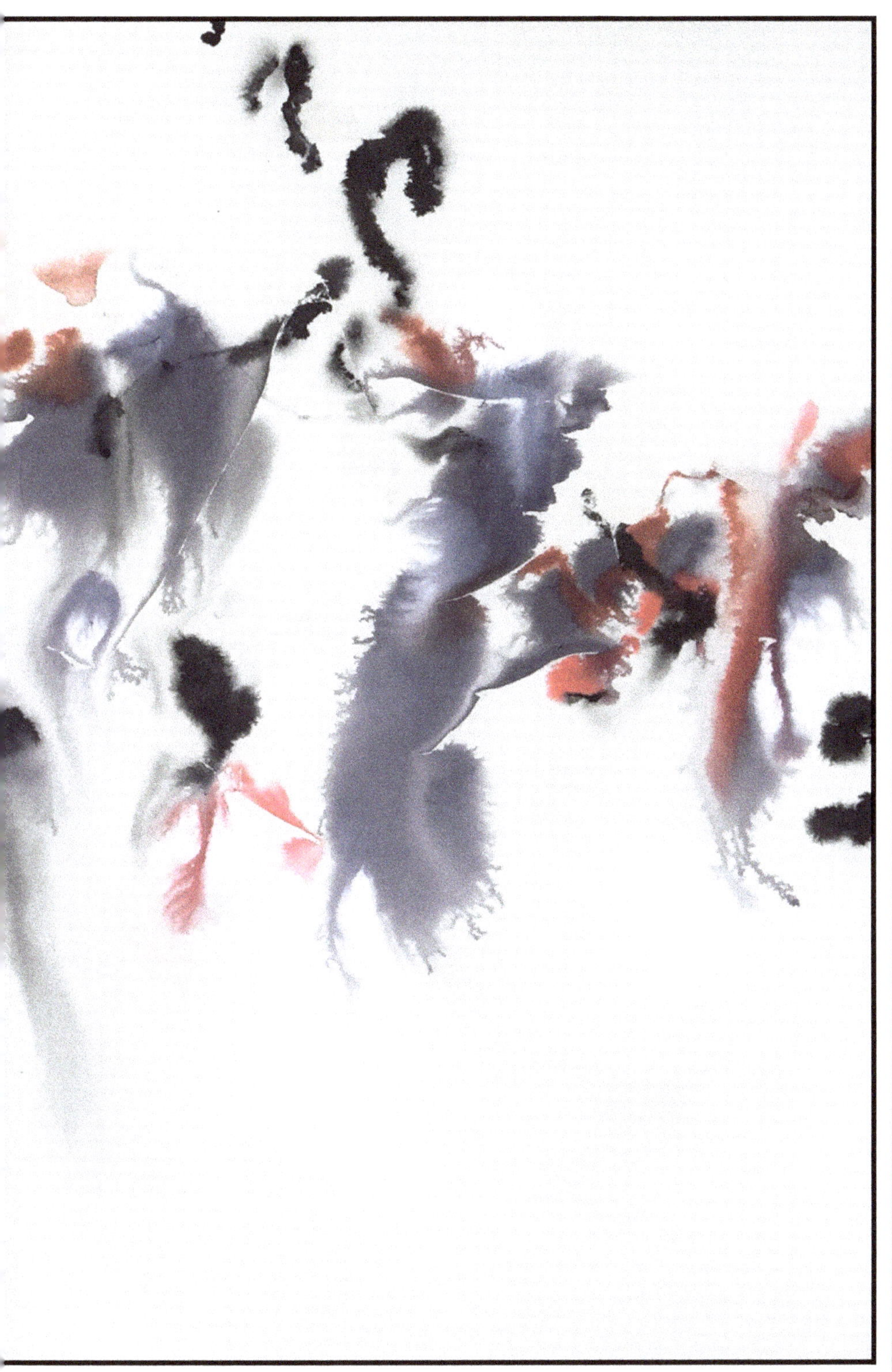

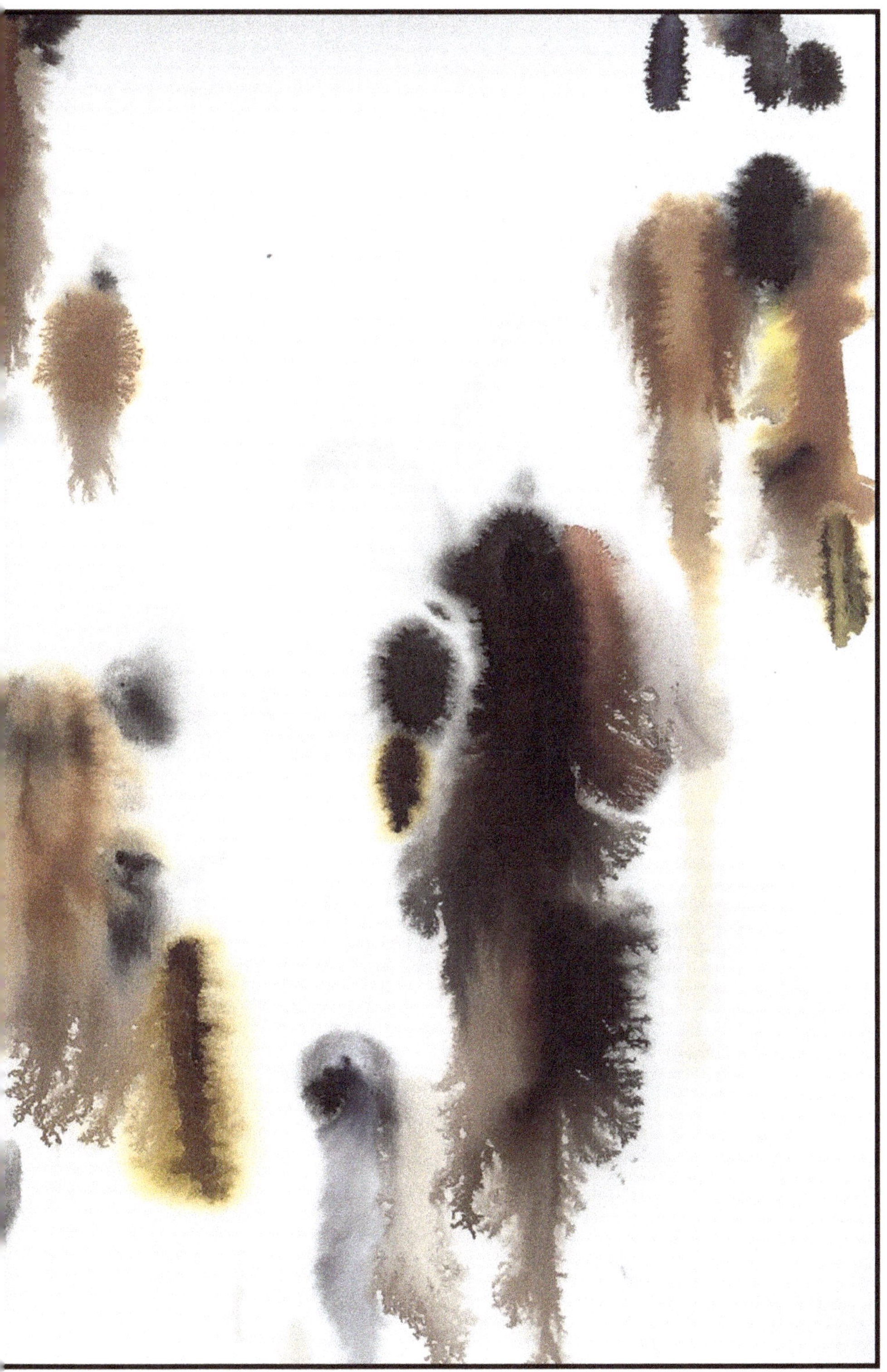

Where Do All Things Go?

Image by Dale Shank

Words by Catherine Marenghi

I think that all things
retain memory:
The Old Town canoe,
solid workhouse of summer days,
remembers bearing yellow dogs
wicker fishing baskets,
wrinkled hands and lithe children.
Here, propped against the old shed,
the outer skin still glints a showy
red, as if to lure the eye away
from broken keel and thwart.
The peeling oars dip into
another season's dried leaves
and fallen twigs. Broken flowerpots,
discarded tires, burst from the leaves
like bobbing fish. The oars no longer
gently pry into the freshwater,
delving in as lovers would.

Where do all things go,
the wreck and ruin,
when they no longer glide or soar?

Where do all things go,
when they are not held aloft
in precious satin-lined boxes
borne on six strong shoulders?
Junkyards for bones or metal parts,
untended cemeteries, weeded over,
landfill or suffocating fire.

The ancient beasts were wiser, simply
dropped where they stood,
to give themselves to silt
or warm amber.

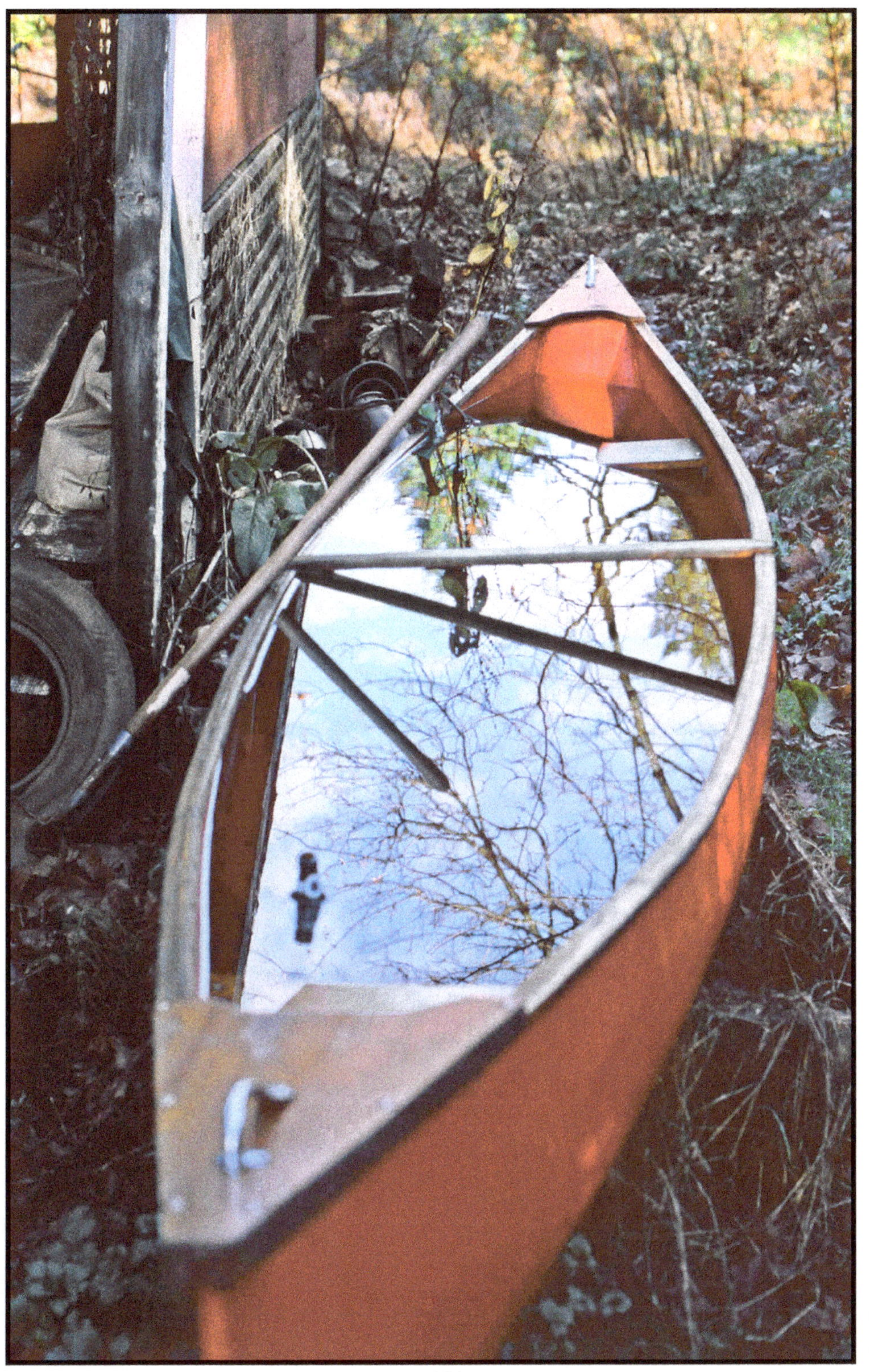

In Order Of Appearance:

Apoorva Prabhakar is an artist, writer, photographer and filmmaker in New York. With an extensive background in fine arts and a penchant for storytelling, she incorporates different mediums to depict stories that resonate with people.

Travis was born and raised on the flatlands of West Texas. He received an MFA from the University of California, Riverside. He currently lives in Kansas City, where he hosts a weekly writers workshop.

Laura Lee is a Chicago area poet, college instructor, literacy tutor, and writer. Her poetry, fiction, and nonfiction have been published in print and online journals in the US, the UK, New Zealand, India, and Greece.
For a complete list of publications, visit her website at: http://lauraleewriterpoeteducator.com.
Follow Laura Lee on Twitter at: https://twitter.com/LauraLe97942016.

Natalia Prusinska is a queer, first generation Polish American poet. She graduated from the University of Rochester with both an Economics and Russian degree. Her poetry has been published in Storm Cellar and elsewhere.
IG: @nataliagodyla

Erika Kari McCarthy is an observer, obsessor, and creator of bodies. She received her BFA in Studio Fine Arts from Rochester Institute of Technology in 2018. She now works to provide uninterrupted time and space for artists from all walks of life as Assistant Manager of the Byrdcliffe Artist Residency in Woodstock, NY.
Her work is driven by material exploration, scientific inquiry, and the repetition of rituals and compulsions. She has been published in print media such as the Toho Journal, The Hand and Signatures Magazine, and featured as the artwork for the TAK Ensemble's latest album (2019). While retaining ties to her origins in upstate New York, Erika currently lives and works as a nomad in no specific geographic location.
instagram : @erikakari

John Leonard is an ELA teacher and poetry editor for Twyckenham Notes. He holds an M.A. in English from Indiana University. His previous works have appeared in Poetry Quarterly, Chiron Review, North Dakota Review, Roanoke Review, Sheila-Na-Gig online, Eclectica Magazine, Rappahannock Review, Mud Season Review, The Blue Mountain Review, Rock & Sling, The Moving Force Journal, Rockvale Review, Trailer Park Quarterly, Genre: Urban Arts, and Burningword Literary Journal. His work is forthcoming in december, Levee Magazine, Unstamatic Magazine, Punt Volat, Stonecoast Review, and The Oakland Review. John was the 2016 inaugural recipient of the Wolfson Poetry Award, the 2018 recipient of the Josephine K. Piercy Memorial Award, and the 2019 recipient of the David E. Albright Memorial Award and Hatfield Merit Award. He lives in Elkhart, Indiana with his wife, three cats, and two dogs. You can follow him on Twitter at @jotyleon and @TwyckenhamNotes.

Emily Shoff has had essays in The New York Times, USA Today, The Denver Post, and in magazines such as High Country News, Trail Runner, and Outside Online. Several of her poems were short listed in the Tom Howard Contest, and her short story "Ghost Crabbing" was published in Red Rock Review. She is currently writing a novel, Save What Remains, the story of a geology professor who lands himself in jail while trying to save Utah's public lands from fracking and of his strong-willed daughter, who sets out to save him. She lives in Telluride, Colorado with her husband and two daughters.
@shofffamilyadventures

Terence Degnan has published two full-length books of poetry. He is a co-director at the Camperdown Organization which was created to increase access to publication and education as well as promote agency for underrepresented writers. He lives in Brooklyn with his wife and daughter.

Moises was born in New York in 1967, but grew up in the island of Puerto Rico. His career started during the late 1980's where his artwork was selected to be exposed in several galleries and collective art shows. After his bachelor's degree in arts (1990) he continued participating in collective expositions, not only in Puerto Rico, but also in the USA, England, France and Europe. His first solo show "De Pared de Colgantes" was held in 1993 at Domus Gallery in San Juan, P. R. Ramos' artwork was selected in 1993 and 1996 for the prestigious Biennial of Latin American & the Caribbean Engravings in San Juan, P.R.
Moises has also received awards for his mixed media, engravings and black & white photography throughout his career. Since 1993, he has been working as an art educator and was selected teacher of the year several times in Puerto Rico. Ramos has been living in Jacksonville, Florida since 2002, where he continues working as an artist and an educator. His devoted work as a teacher with his students and the community deemed him the recipient of the Memphis Wood Excellence in Teaching Award in 2009. Later in 2010he received the Cultural Council of Jacksonville Art Educator of the Year Award for his volunteer work and community outreach projects with refugee students. He has participated in numerous art expositions locally and internationally and is still striving to create meaningful artworks every day.
Web portfolio: https://moisesramos.wixsite.com/fine-art
Web Store: https://moises-ramos.pixels.com
Instagram: https://www.instagram.com/mramosfineart/
Facebook: https://www.facebook.com/Mramosfineart/

Kate MacDonald is a septuagenarian insomniac who says she is grateful for the extra time to play. In the last few months Kate decided it was time to put her fingers to the keyboard again and let someone other than herself read what she has delighted in creating. She feels that anyone who writes will understand what she means when she says "Sometimes an idea suddenly appears and the compulsion is so strong to run with it that it almost seems to write itself"
Kate enjoys writing poetry and she is working on two more books, one is about the paranormal and the other features demons and ghosts. Deep subjects perhaps but as always there is a vein of humour running throughout.
Kate has now retired. She started work at Fifteen and a half years old in Electronics refurbishing Gyroscopic Gunsights used in Spitfires, left work to bring up her children then returned to work at Thirty Eight to eventually head the Technical Department at Sky TV in the good old Analogue days. At the moment she dabbles in buying junk and selling "Antiques" as well as reviving her Seventies interest in Macramé, (Knotty) also String 'n Pin Art (Painful) which she finds as much fun as she remembers.

Joanna Acevedo received her BA in Literary Studies from the New School in 2019. She currently studies Fiction at New York University, where she is working on her MFA. Her work has been seen in or is forthcoming in Track Four, Mikrokosmos, Not Very Quiet, and Pangyrus Magazine, among others. She is a Hospitalfield 2020 Interdisciplinary Resident, Goldwater Fellow, Prose Editor at Inklette Magazine and teaches creative writing at NYU. She can be found on Instagram at @joavocado.

Lino Azevedo was born in the 1970s to Portuguese immigrants near the city of San Francisco, California. Like most small children, Lino enjoyed creating from the soul with simple tools like pencil and crayon. Being a painter herself, his mother saw the potential and let him try his hand with her oils and brushes. After receiving an art award in high school, a counselor suggested San Jose State University for its strong art and design program. Lino graduated in 1997 with his bachelors and began teaching drawing and painting to both children and adults. With a growing passion for guiding other artists on their journeys, he decided to pursue his MFA in order to teach. In 2013, he received his MFA from Winthrop University. Lino teaches foundations studies at Savannah College of Art and Design. His work has been shown in galleries throughout North America.
@azevedofineart

Levi DeMatteo is a Chicago based multimedia artist whose practice includes but is not limited to detailed ink illustrations, bizarre mockumentaries, digital photo collages, and a plethora of musical projects. Whether watched, heard, or looked at, his work consistently opens portals to surreal (and often absurd) worlds rendered with dizzying attention to detail. He graduated with distinctions from The School Of The Art Institute of Chicago where he studied video and audio production. He has exhibited work in The Katonah Museum of Art, Sullivan Galleries, Lucid Film Fest, and The Gene Siskel Film Center.
insta: @starfish_hospital

Mugu Ganesan is an emerging poet based out of Minneapolis, Minnesota. He writes poetry in English and Urdu. His poetry has appeared or is forthcoming in The Hindu, Burning House Press, and Scarlet Leaf Review. He has participated in poetry workshops at the UCLA Extension and The Loft Literary Center. Mugu's poetry is focused on expressing the strife that comes with being human through his observations and life experiences across cultures and continents.

Matt Vekakis is a poet, painter & educator. His work has been published or is forthcoming in Cathexis Northwest Press, Tule Review, Peregrine Journal, Gravitas, Poached Hare, Waccamaw, Inklette Magazine & A Midwestern Review, among others. He lives with his beau in Northampton, MA—teaching 11th grade English at a local high school. You can keep up with him at @mattvekakis.

Jessica Manack lives in Pittsburgh and holds degrees from Hollins University. She has been published in Prime Number Magazine and The Pittsburgh Post-Gazette, and has toured as part of the Perpetual Motion Roadshow.   Follow her at @jessicamanack

Emory Schuett, at the age of thirty-one, has faced many obstacles and triumphed. At fourteen, he plunged into psychosis. Before that, he was what most would say a typical kid—obsessing over Final Fantasy, playing racquetball at the court down the street, riding bikes along the canal, writing, watching Anime, and hiking in the desert with his father. After, he was anything but typical. Often, the psychosis persisted for more than half the day, and, at one point, he was stripped of all that he loved. He could no longer even enjoy a television show, listen to music, or attend school. His own mind kept him from his joys, but it also unveiled a world unknown before. Laws of physics were bent, colors became tastes, tastes became textures, and with the horror came beauty. Since then and many hospitalizations, many medicinal cocktails, he has sunk and emerged from the darkest of the psychosis over and over again. Each time, in its wake, he has found his art.

Andi Talbot is a 30-year-old writer and performance poet from Newcastle, England
He has been recently published in Bonnie's Crew (#5, Oct 2019) Paper and Ink Zine (#15, Nov 2019) and Fragmented Voices (March 2020).
His debut collection, "Burn Before Reading" is available now via Analog Submission Press.
In his free time he enjoys reading, drinking rum and getting lost in unfamiliar cities.

Dustin Hyman is dyslexic and supports nuerodiversity. He's been a freelance writer and a journalist. Now, after earning a PhD in Creative Writing from the University of Louisiana, Dustin finds himself teaching English at a tiny college in Colorado. He's designed two book covers and his photography continues to appear in shady places...

Tony is a self taught artist who's work has been in over 75 Nationwide and Regional juried art shows and exhibits. All of the images you see are made using bits of junk and recycled plastics. Tony then takes these creations to out of the norm and unique settings so that they can be photographed and transformed into the "Otherworldly." If you look closely at his work you might recognize some common household items.

Avleen K Mokha holds a B.A. in English Literature and Linguistics from McGill University. She is the 2019 winner of McGill's Peterson Memorial Prize for Creative Writing. Avleen's work has appeared in journals such Déraciné Magazine, Dream Pop, and Yolk Literary. Avleen edits poetry and prose for Persephone's Daughters, a literary magazine devoted to survivors of abuse. Presently, Avleen works as a journalist in Montreal and focuses on covering under-reported communities. Her first poetry chapbook, DREAM FRAGMENTS, is forthcoming this autumn by Cactus Press.

Jonathan Douglas Duran is a ____________ , ____________ and ____________ .
He is the recipient of the _______________ and won the _______________ for his work on
_________________ .
He resides in ____________ with his _______________ .
He is currently ______________________________________ .

Marieken Cochius is a Dutch-born artist who has lived and worked in New York City since 1987, and in the Hudson Valley since 2013. Meditative, strong and intuitive work that often explores growth forms, movement and containment of energy, she is drawn to remote places where she studies nature and makes art inspired by it. Her work encompasses drawing, painting, sculpture and printmaking. A sculptural public commission was completed in 2017 for the Village of Wappingers Falls, NY. Recent solo shows were at Matteawan Gallery in Beacon, NY, and Holland Tunnel Gallery in Brooklyn, NY. Cochius' work has been exhibited in numerous galleries and institutions in places ranging from New York City, NY, Berkeley, CA, Austin, TX, Los Angeles, CA, to Japan, Germany and the Netherlands. Her work is in numerous private collections in the US and Europe. She has participated in residencies including the Vermont Studio Center, Johnson, VT. Cochius has participated in recent group exhibitions at The Ely Center, New Haven, CT; Ann Street Gallery, Newburgh, NY; LAB Space, Hillsdale, NY; Sideshow Gallery, Brooklyn, NY; Ube Gallery, Berkeley, CA. Her work has been recently featured in on covers of Willard and Maple Magazine, Sun Spot Journal, and inside of Esthetic Apostle, FLAR, DeLuge Journal, Alluvian Environmental Journal, Raw Art Review.
https://www.instagram.com/mariekencochius/
@mariekencochius

Dale Shank's assignment photography includes performance art, wildlife, environmental documentation, and professional pool players. His fiction and poetry have been published in: Exquisite Corpse, The Raw Art Review, Akros Review, Before the Sun, Croton Review, Joint Endeavor, Powder, and University of Portland Review.

A native of Massachusetts, the granddaughter of Italian immigrants, Catherine Marenghi is the author of "Breaking Bread: Poems" (Finishing Line Press, 2020). An award-winning poet, she received first-place honors in separate contests judged by acclaimed poets Richard Blanco and Jennifer Clement. Her poems also twice received first-place honors from the Academy of American Poets University and College Poetry Prize program. Her work has appeared in literary journals in the U.S. and Mexico, including Cider Press Review, Sisyphus, Peregrine Journal, Crossroads, Solamente en San Miguel, Italian Americana, Mobius: The Journal of Social Change, Phi Kappa Phi Forum, and Conclave. She also authored "Glad Farm: A Memoir" (Tate Publishing, 2016), a story of stark poverty and resilience, set on a former gladiolus farm. President Jimmy Carter called it "inspiring." She holds an M.A., B.A. summa cum laude in English from Tufts University, where she studied with Denise Levertov and X.J. Kennedy, and currently divides her time between Cape Cod, Massachusetts, and San Miguel de Allende, Mexico.
Instagram: @CMarenghi
Facebook: facebook.com/GladFarm
Twitter: Marenghi
www.marenghi.com

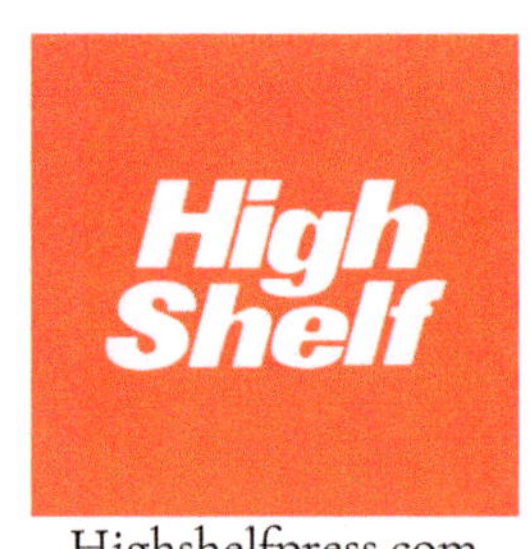

Highshelfpress.com